BANJO PATERSON

Also by Derek Parker:

The Fall of Phaethon (1954)

Company of Two (with Paul Casimir, 1955)

Beyond Wisdom (verse play, 1957)

Byron and his World (1968)

The Twelfth Rose (ballet libretto, 1969)

The Question of Astrology (1970)

The Westcountry (1973)

John Donne and his World (1975)

Familiar to All: William Lilly and 17th century astrology (1975)

Radio: the great years (1977)

The Westcountry and the Sea (1980)

The Memoirs of Cora Pearl (fiction, as William Blatchford, 1983)

God of the Dance: Vaslav Nijinsky (1988)

The Trade of Angels (fiction, 1988)

The Royal Academy of Dancing: the first 75 years (1995)

Writing Erotic Fiction (1995)

Nell Gwyn (2000)

Roman Murder Mystery: the true story of Pompilia (2001)

Casanova (2002)

Benvenuto Cellini (2004)

Voltaire (2005)

Outback (2007, paperback published 2009 by Woodslane Press)

Arthur Phillip (2009, Woodslane Press)

Governor Macquarie (2010, Woodslane Press)

Building Sydney's History (with Julia Parker, 2011, Woodslane Press)

THE MAN WHO WROTE

BANJO PATERSON

DEREK PARKER

WOODSLANE

Woodslane Press Pty Ltd
7/5 Vuko Place, Warriewood, NSW 2102
Email: info@woodslane.com.au
Website: www.woodslane.com.au

© 2010 Woodslane Press, text © 2009 and 2010 Derek Parker

National Library of Australia Cataloguing-in-Publication entry

Author:	Parker, Derek.
Title:	Banjo Paterson : the man who wrote Waltzing Matilda : his life and poetry / Derek Parker.
Edition:	1st ed.
ISBN:	9781921683473 (pbk.)
Notes:	Bibliography.
Subjects:	Paterson, A. B. (Andrew Barton), 1864-1941.
	Poets, Australian--Biography.
	Australian poetry--19th century.
	Ballads, English--Australia.
Dewey Number:	A821.2

Design and layout by Vanessa Wilton, Billy Boy Design
Printed in China

For Ann Tomlinson
with love

Contents

Foreword

A. B. Paterson, known in Australia – and indeed throughout the English-speaking world – as 'Banjo' Paterson, was an adventurous man whose life largely lacked adventure. Apart from his months in South Africa as correspondent of the *Sydney Morning Herald* during the Boer War, his attempts to find excitement mostly failed. His efforts to get to the front as a war correspondent during the first European war failed, and a potentially exciting journey through China and Siberia to Russia petered out.

This by no means suggests that his life was a failure or a disappointment. It was far from it. He was a popular journalist and broadcaster, and on a personal level a distinguished man of the turf and a fine rider and polo player with a comprehensive knowledge of horses and horse-flesh. His family life was placid and happy. Apart from this, he wrote what was to become his nation's unofficial national anthem.

A detailed account of his life would involve – has involved, in the two biographies previously written of him – a great deal of material of relatively little interest to the general reader, except when it is related in Paterson's own often vivid, humorous and racy prose. So to a large extent this is a biography which is almost an autobiography, for I have quoted from his writing rather more than would otherwise be customary. To turn into one's own prose, for instance, The Banjo's accounts of the Boer War and the men he met in South Africa, or of the war hospital in which he briefly served during the first great European war, would be to lose his own tone of voice, which is the man himself. It would not be too much to compare his best dispatches with those sent to London from the Zulu War a generation earlier, by perhaps the greatest of all war correspondents, William Russell of *The Times*.

His records of the war, together with his other journalism and complete poems, were collected in over fifteen hundred pages in two enormous volumes, published in 1983 and edited by his two grand-daughters, Rosamund Campbell and Philippa Harvie. These volumes, which also contain important appendices, are not only a tribute to Paterson and to the assiduous work of the editors, but a symbol of family loyalty and respect.

'The Banjo' (as he almost always signed himself), was modest about his verse, which he never referred to as poetry. 'Poetry', he once wrote, 'is older than civilisation, possibly older than speech, and it will make men laugh or love or weep or fight better than any acting or any speech-making. Of course, this only applies to real poetry, and not to the verse that most of us write. There is a great difference between poetry and verse, and when a man speaks of real poetry he should always take his hat off.'

Later, in a retrospective essay for the *Sydney Mail* in December 1938, he spoke of his verse and that of his friend and contemporary Henry Lawson:

> Our 'ruined rhymes' are not likely to last long, but if there is any hope at all of survival it comes from the fact that such writers as Lawson and myself had the advantage of writing in a new country. In all museums throughout the world one may see plaster casts of the footprints of weird animals, footprints preserved for posterity, not because the animals were particularly good of their sort, but because they had the luck to walk on the lava while it was cooling. There is just a faint hope that something of the same sort may happen to us.

Introduction

In the summer of 1895, not long after Christmas, A. B. Paterson, a 31-year-old Sydney solicitor, journalist and writer of ballads, went off to spend a break with his fiancée, Sarah Riley, at the home of her brother Frederick at Winton in Queensland. There they met up with Christina and Jean Macpherson, two sisters who with their father were on their way to join their brother Robert at Dagworth Station on the Diamantina River. Christina and Sarah were old school friends, and the Macphersons invited the two travellers to spend some time at Dagworth. They happily agreed.

Dagworth was about 130 kilometres from Winton, almost 1400 kilometres north-west of Brisbane, in harsh, drought-prone country first settled in the 1860s. Winton was originally named Pelican Waterhole, a mere dot on the map known only to Burke and Wills and those who later followed in their footsteps. It had become an important transportation point for the cattle and sheep stations of the area, also used by Robert Macpherson and his brothers at Dagworth Station.

The family welcomed their sisters' friends, and Paterson, an excellent horseman, was soon riding out around the property with Robert. He had a quick ear for stories of the bush – and heard several from his host. For instance the 'Battle of Dagworth' three months or so earlier, when striking shearers fought with the Macphersons, and one of them, Samuel 'French' Hoffmeister who, rather than be arrested, committed suicide beside the Combo Waterhole near Kynuna. Then there were the tales of a swagman and stockman, Harry Wood, who had beaten an Aboriginal boy to death, and was found by three policemen sitting by a billabong, and of a drunken scourer who had fallen into the waterhole and drowned ...

These ingredients were matched in some mysterious way with an old Scottish tune Christina had heard a local band play at the Warrnambool races some time before, and which she played to the family one evening on the autoharp which was the only musical instrument at the Macphersons' house. Paterson reached for a piece of paper and began to scribble:

> *Oh! There once was a swagman camped in a*
> > *Billabong*
> *Under the shade of a Coolabah tree ...*

Not only was 'Waltzing Matilda' born that evening at Dagworth. So was the immortality of Banjo Paterson.

ONE

Childhood in the Bush

Andrew Barton Paterson was born on 17 February 1864 at Narambla, on the northern side of the town of Orange, in New South Wales. His father, also Andrew, was a Scot who had emigrated to Australia when he was sixteen, with his brother John and their sister. They took up the squatting run of Buckinbah at Obley, near Yeoval, not far from Dubbo and the present site of the Western Plains zoo. Seventy years later, Banjo wrote about Buckinbah in recollections for the *Sydney Morning Herald*:

> This place was held on a lease from the Crown at a few pence per acre and was worth no more. It was dingo-infested, unfenced country where the sheep had to be shepherded and the cattle, as the blackboys said could go 'longa bush' and wander afield until they got into somebody else's meat cask or could be mustered and driven away by enterprising people who adopted this cheap method of stocking-up.[1]

Apart from that, it was a battle for the brothers to make a go of their sheep station in arid scrubland, but Andrew was at least confident enough of the future to court and marry Rose Barton, the daughter of a couple who ran another station, Boree Nyrang, near Cudal, forty kilometres west of Orange, in Cabonne country, now a pleasant small town in the middle of prosperous farming land. Rose's mother, Emily, was a strong and intelligent woman who had been educated in Europe and had literary tastes – which were subjugated to domestic life at Boree Nyrang, where over twenty-five years, she bore and brought up nine children.

Emily's life was not an easy one in many ways. There were the harsh living conditions, (no worse than those of many neighbours), and occasional dangers such as the time she and her children cowered in a back room while members of the local Aboriginal tribe stripped the house bare of food. As for her husband Robert, he was lame, irritable and incompetent, and money was in short supply.

But the family survived, more than survived, for the indomitable Emily was not only largely responsible for running the station, but with the aid of an occasional governess, saw to her children's education. There is a story that while at the kitchen table making bread, she would have them stand around her, reciting Latin verbs.

Andrew and Rose were married at the station as there was no church within easy reach. It was one of the last times there was a family gathering there, for in 1860 Robert Barton suddenly died. Emily sold Boree Nyrang and with the capital bought a small house in Sydney – an 1830s 'cottage' originally built as an inn, but never used as such - and moved there.

Andrew and Rose set up home at Buckinbah with brother John, but when Rose fell pregnant, they were concerned at the remoteness of the station, and it was decided that she should have her child at an aunt's house at Narambla, with a doctor within easy reach at Orange. And it was there that Rose's son, always known to the family as 'Barty', was born.

His mother and aunt were devoted to him, and he was well looked after though at some time, probably before he could walk, he was dropped by a servant and broke his arm. No-one realised this until he was ten, when he had a fall which further damaged the bones. More falls – usually from horses, for he was rarely out of the saddle – compounded the trouble, and for the whole of his life he suffered from stiffness and weakness in his right arm, and particularly his hand.

Barty's father was largely absent from Buckinbah, striving to make a living in hard times and hard places. Drought was endemic – in 1869 a day was set aside for 'general humiliation and prayer' in the idle hope of breaking it - and this and low prices drove Andrew from the Buckinbah property to work as far away as Queensland, where he bought richer land at Stainburn Downs. On aAt least on one occasion he drove his sheep there overland from the New South Wales station, and once was caught on flooded country between two rivers and had to shear them on a sandhill, losing the wool. Eventually he was forced to sell his Queensland property, at a serious financial loss.

Unaware of all this, Barty lived an idyllic life, sometimes at Narambla in his great-aunt's cottage surrounded by an 'English' garden planted with roses, wall-flowers and lavender; but more often at Buckinbah. Eventually he lived in even more remote bush country, for his father was finally driven to bankruptcy:

> *... droughts and losses came apace*
> *Till ruin stared him in the face;*
> *He toiled and toiled while lived the light,*
> *He dreamed of overdrafts at night:*
> *At length, because he could not pay,*
> *His bankers took the stock away.*[2]

Andrew had to sell his station and bought a smaller property, Illalong, near Yass. Once more he was forced to sell up – but the buyer, Henry Brown, who owned other properties nearby, made him his manager, and Andrew, Rose and Barty were able to stay at Illalong station, near Yass, in the bushland which the boy came to love and celebrate in verse:

> *A land as far as the eye can see, where the*
>   *waving grasses grow*
> *Or the plains are blackened and burnt and*
>   *bare, where the false mirages go*
> *Like shifting symbols of hope deferred - land*
>   *where you never know.*
> *Land of plenty or land of want, where the grey*
>   *Companions dance,*
> *Feast or famine, or hope or fear, and in all*
>   *things land of chance,*
> *Where Nature pampers or Nature slays, in her*
>   *ruthless, red, romance.*
> *And we catch a sound of a fairy's song, as the*
>   *wind goes whipping by,*

Or a scent like incense drifts along from the
herbage ripe and dry
- Or the dust storms dance on their ballroom
floor, where the bones of the cattle lie.[3]

Eventually, the family was to be enlarged by the arrival of a younger brother and five sisters – but the first of Barty's siblings was not born until he was twelve, so his formative early childhood was solitary. The result was a quickening of his imagination and the awakening of a delight in the life of the bush around him, which never left him. The move from Buckinbah to Illalong was in many ways a blessing, for while the former was genuinely a place in which nothing ever happened, the latter was in much more interesting country. Illalong was also on the main road between Sydney and Melbourne, along which there was a continual stream of fascinating traffic. In his reminiscences Paterson described his childhood there:

There were swimming pools in the creek 10 feet deep and half a mile long, horses to ride, and the tides of life surged round us. The gold escort from Lambing Flat, too, came by twice a week, with a mounted trooper riding in front with his rifle at the ready and another armed trooper on the box with the coachman. I used to hope that the escort would be 'stuck up' outside our place so that I might see something worth while, but what with the new settlers and the scores of bullock teams taking loading out to the back country, no bushranger stood half a chance of making a getaway unseen.

The roads were quite unmade, and when the track got so cut up that a wagon would sink down to its axles, the bullockies would try a new track. Thus the highway became a labyrinth of tracks, half a mile wide, with here and there an excavation where a wagon had been dug out; and when, as often happened, a wagon got stuck in the bed of the creek, they would hitch two teams of bullockies to it, and then (as one of the bullockies said) either the wagon or the bed of the creek had to come.

I was not encouraged to go anywhere near the bullockies, who were supposed to be up to stratagems and spoils, especially in the way of stealing horses; but a lonely child will go anywhere for company, and I found that they travelled with their families, dogs, and sometimes even fowls. These latter gentry, after fossicking about the camp for worms and grasshoppers, would hop up into the wagon as soon as the bullocks were yoked, making for their crate, where a little food awaited them. They hurried too![4]

In due course it was time for Barty to go to school. He had learned to ride as soon as he could keep his seat on a pony, and rode over every day to the little bush school at Binalong, four miles from home, where the Irish schoolmaster raised kangaroo dogs, bred gamecocks and organised cock-fighting. The regime there would not be recognised by any five-year-old schoolboy today:

> Carlyle in his 'Sartor Resartus' speaks of his hero Diogenes Teudelsdrock as being educated at the Academy of Hinterschlag (stern-smackers), and there was plenty of Hinterschlag at this little bush school in Binalong. The master, Moore by name, had to meet emergencies of one sort or another every day, and he met them like Napoleon. Spare, gaunt, and Irish by descent, he ran to gamecocks and kangaroo dogs in his private moments. It was nothing unusual for his flock to go out with him in the long

summer afternoons to watch a course after a kangaroo, and the elite of the school, the pound-keeper's son and the blacksmith's boy, would be allowed to stop after school and watch a 'go-in' between two cocks without the steel spurs, as part of their training for more serious business.

One day, I remember, the sergeant of police from Yass, in plain clothes, drove up to the door of the school in a natty little trap with a pair of ponies. We jumped to the conclusion that he had heard of this cockfighting business, and we expected (and hoped) to see the schoolmaster led away like Eugene Aram with gyves upon his wrist. While the sergeant was inside with the teacher we children swarmed all over his buggy, and there in a neat lattice-lined box under the seat we found a gamecock, clipped and looking for a fight! The gamecock was rather surprised to see us in charge of his caravan, but not nearly so astonished as we were to see *him*.[5]

How much Barty actually learned, academically, at the bush school is doubtful, but he certainly learned a lot about bush life from the other boys around him. Most arrived like him either on ponies or on foot from shacks and stations miles away. The schoolmaster no doubt taught them something aside from cockfighting, but was no stickler for school routine, and survived in his position thanks to a careful system of spies which warned him when a school inspector was approaching. He was never completely cured of his addiction to the cane, despite a number of school visits by the fierce mothers of some of the boys he assaulted. There was a woman teacher too, but Paterson never mentions her.

The house at Illalong had originally consisted of just four large rooms and a couple of small ones were added. Then Barty's parents bought another four-roomed house, and brought it to Illalong jacked up on rollers. He always remembered his first sight of it, swaying like a ship at sea as it was pulled through the trees by a team of bullocks (the two leading ones, Rodney and Spot, became his admired personal friends).

Horses were to be almost the most important part of his life – certainly as far as recreation was concerned, but also during his service in the 1914-18 war. He came to racing very early. One New Year's Day when he was eight year old, an 18-year-old general workman on the station went off to the races at Bogolong (now Bookham), on the Hume Highway. The original racetrack is preserved as an open paddock a short distance from the village, which in 1872 consisted solely of two pubs half a mile apart. When Barty asked his friend where the rest of the town was, the roustabout replied: 'This is all they is. One pub to ketch the coves coming from Yass and the other to ketch the coves from Jugiong.'

The scene must have been wildly exciting for the boy – hundreds of horses hitched to young gum-trees or bushes growing in the scrub, ridden to the races from as far away as the Murrumbidgee mountains and the Snowy River, each it seemed, with a dog nipping at its heels. The men were as rough as their horses – 'blackfellows and half-castes from everywhere, and a few out-and-outers who had ridden down from Lobb's Hole, a place so steep that (as the horse-boy said) the horses all wore the hair off their tails sliding down the mountains.' There was a sprinkling too of 'more civilised sportsmen' from Yass and Jugiong, interested in the horses, but more interested in the gambling.

The main race of the afternoon was the Bogolong Town Plate – a mile race open to any horse a rider wanted to enter. As the entrants were saddling up, Barty was surprised to see a man taking the saddle off the pony he had ridden over, and putting it on another horse. He ran over. 'That's my saddle!' he protested. 'Right-oh, son,' said the man – 'I won't hurt it. It's just the very thing the doctor ordered ... this is the lightest saddle here, so I took it before anybody else got it.' He patted the horse on the flank. 'This is Pardon,' he said, 'and after he wins his heat you come to me and I'll stand you a bottle of ginger beer.'

Barty could scarcely contain his excitement as he watched the horses disappear into the scrub in one confused bunch, Pardon somewhere at the back – and saw as they came into view again, that he was lying third in the field. Once in the straight, Pardon romped home – then led the field in the second heat, and under the rules of the race won the cup.

'I had the ginger-beer,' Paterson remembered as an adult – 'bitter, luke-warm stuff with hops in it - but what did I care? My new friend assured me that Pardon could not have won without my saddle. It had made all the difference. Years afterwards, I worked the incident into a sort of ballad called *Pardon, the son of Reprieve*.[6]

When he was ten, Barty's mother and grandmother decided that it was time he went to a proper school. An unexpected bequest enabled Rose to send him to Sydney Grammar School – as a day-boy, for happily his grandmother Emily was able to give him a home at Gladesville. For five months he had preparatory coaching by a tutor at a private house where, he recorded wryly, 'we were all young gentlemen, and had to wear good clothes instead of hob-nailed boots and moleskins', and reluctantly learn to dance.[7]

The Grammar School had sprung from a 'public free grammar school' opened in 1825 with Laurence Hynes Halloran as headmaster. Halloran had fled to Australia from England where he had been accused of immorality, had piled up unpaid debts, and (as it turned out) had awarded himself the degrees in Divinity of which he boasted. A 'Sydney College' followed this in 1830, operating in one large room (which is still in use, known as 'Big School') in a building in Hyde Park, but lasted for only twenty years, and it was in 1857 that Sydney Grammar School proper opened. Barty attended it for six years, which seem neither to have been specially happy or unhappy. Study centred on English, Latin, Greek and mathematics. He was good at the first, enjoyed the second, found Greek difficult and was competent in maths. School records do not record him as a great scholar – he shared one prize, matriculated when he was sixteen, but failed the university scholarship examination.

As with most schools of the time, Sydney Grammar was not a place for the over-sensitive – there was considerable largely undeterred violence. Barty remembered one bare-fist fight between two boys which went on all the dinner-hour, then again after school, until the boys could hardly stand and had to be held up to continue battering each other. He wrote too of indulging in 'wallarooing', in which small gangs of boys would fall on some other whose only offence was that he was not a sportsman, and at the very least cram grass into his mouth, stamp on his hat and throw his boots away. If this stopped short of positive bullying, it was perhaps not by far, and there is some indication that Paterson rather enjoyed it. His participation in rough and tumble was very possibly a defence mechanism. He was already beginning to write in the school magazine, and would have been eager to not be regarded as a swot – especially as he was not physically equipped to be good at sport (though he did play cricket for the school team and at Illalong when he was home on holiday). His disability was a real one: at one time his thumb was operated on, and it was even thought it might have to be amputated. Fortunately this was avoided, but he was always somewhat self-conscious about it. It did not, however, hamper his horsemanship, which soon became notable. Indeed, he always said that the weakness of his arm made his handling of the bridle more sensitive, and certainly among the cousins and friends with whom he went camping along the Murrumbidgee and in the Snowy River country, he was the most agile and adept rider.

Outside school hours, at home in Gladesville he lived pretty much the usual life of an adolescent boy. He and his cousin Jack bought an old boat – 'mostly held together by tar', he later said:

> By way of brightening up the colour scheme
> we painted the floor with white paint over the
> tar. This was not entirely satisfactory, as the
> tar turned the paint to a sort of unwholesome

> muddy colour, which refused to dry; so we
> had to buy caustic soda to remove both tar
> and paint and begin all over again. When we
> got her finished she was a fine fishing boat,
> for there was generally as much water inside
> as out, which kept our fish fresh till we got
> them home.[8]

They moored the boat at the bottom of the garden which ran down to the water's edge from Rockend Stone Cottage, his grandmother's house. In it, they went fishing, and also hung about with the 'scullers' who raced a course on the Parramatta. Sculling was the major Australian sport until the First World War, the great scullers drawn from the many watermen who earned their living on the Parramatta and the northern rivers of New South Wales — and the headquarters of the Sydney Rowing Club was at Abbotsford, just across the river from Rockend. Apart from bobbing about in their half-waterlogged boat and getting in the way of training scullers, Paterson and his friends were among the huge crowds who watched the sport. It was reckoned that over a hundred thousand people watched major races, travelling by special trains from as far away as Goulburn and Bathurst. Barty and his friends hero-worshipped such giants of the game as Ned Trickett, Elias Laycock — who, they whispered, could eat a dozen eggs for breakfast — and the great Harry Searle, whose funeral cortège was attended by 170,000 people when he died in 1889.

Another, less attractive interest he and Edward had was in dog-fighting — to the extent indeed that they are said to have bought and trained a fighting dog. Later, in an article for the Sydney *Bulletin* written in 1895, he described an illegal meeting:

> Nearly everyone has seen dogs fight ... But an
> ordinary worry between (say) a retriever and
> a collie, terminating as soon as one or other
> gets his ear bitten, gives a very faint idea of a
> real dog-fight. Bull-terriers are the gladiators
> of the canine race. Bred and trained to fight,
> carefully exercised and dieted for weeks

beforehand, they come to the fray exulting in their strength and determined to win. Each is trained to fight for certain holds, a grip of the ear or the back of the neck being of very slight importance. The foot is a favourite hold, the throat is, of course, fashionable - if they can get it.

The white and the brindle sparred and wrestled and gripped and threw each other, fighting grimly, and disdaining to utter a sound. Their seconds dodged round them unceasingly, giving them encouragement and advice – 'That's the style, Boxer - fight for his foot' – 'Draw your foot back, old man,' and so on. Now and again one dog got a grip of the other's foot and chewed savagely, and the spectators danced with excitement. The moment the dogs let each other go they were snatched up by their seconds and carried to their corners, and a minute's time was allowed, in which their mouths were washed out and a cloth rubbed over their bodies.

Then came the ceremony of 'coming to scratch'. When time was called for the second round the brindled dog was let loose in his own corner, and was required by the rules to go across the ring of his own free will and attack the other dog. If he failed to do this he would lose the fight. The white dog, meanwhile, was held in his corner waiting the attack. After the next round it was the white dog's turn to make the attack, and so on alternately. The animals need not fight a moment longer than they chose, as either dog could abandon the fight by failing to attack his enemy.

While their condition lasted they used to dash across the ring at full run; but, after a while, when the punishment got severe and their 'fitness' began to fail, it became a very exciting question whether or not a dog would 'come to scratch'. The brindled dog's condition was not so good as the other's. He used to lie on his stomach between the rounds to rest himself, and several times it looked as if he would not cross the ring when his turn came. But as soon as time was called he would start to his feet and limp slowly across glaring steadily at his adversary; then, as he got nearer, he would quicken his pace, make a savage rush, and in a moment they would be locked in combat. So they battled on for fifty-six minutes, till the white dog (who was apparently having all the best of it), on being called to cross the ring, only went half-way across and stood there for a minute growling savagely. So he lost the fight.

No doubt it was a brutal exhibition. But it was not cruel to the animals in the same sense that pigeon-shooting or hare-hunting is cruel. The dogs are born fighters, anxious and eager to fight, desiring nothing better. Whatever limited intelligence they have is all directed to this one consuming passion. They could stop when they liked, but anyone looking on could see that they gloried in the combat. Fighting is like breath to them - they must have it. Nature has implanted in all animals a fighting instinct for the weeding out of the physically unfit, and these dogs have an extra share of that fighting instinct.

Of course, now that militarism is going to be abolished, and the world is going to be so good and teetotal, and only fight in debating societies, these nasty savage animals will be out of date. We will not be allowed to keep anything more quarrelsome than a poodle -

and a man of the future, the New Man, whose
fighting instincts have not been quite bred out
of him, will, perhaps, be found at grey dawn
of a Sunday morning with a crowd of other
unregenerates in some backyard frantically
cheering two of them to mortal combat.[9]

Excursions to dog-fights and other pleasures were one thing but
quite another were Emily Barton's efforts to civilise Barty – a
much more important role, one might guess, than was played
by any of his schoolmasters. She was a writer of verse, and kept
a summerhouse in the garden in which to write. She spoke with
him in French, she enthused about the work of Ruskin, Carlyle
and Swinburne so enthusiastically that he actually read them.
(The swinging metres of Swinburne's poems had a clear effect on
the verse he was already trying to write). The friends who came
to Mrs Barton's evening parties were intelligent and cultured,
and their conversational habits and natural ease of behaviour
rubbed off on the boy who was rapidly becoming a young man.

But it was not only European culture that he learned
from his grandmother; she had after all, spent a lot of her life in
the bush, and she talked to him about that too. She spoke about
the hardships and the rewards, never letting him forget his roots
there, making sure that he always remembered that no amount
of speaking French or reading English poets could impinge on
the fact that first and last he was Australian, only a couple of
generations from those pioneers who had settled the country.

Meanwhile, there was a considerable problem about
Barty's future. Henry Brown, Andrew Paterson's employer,
suddenly died – and with him died the generous promise he
had made to contribute to the boy's education. This was quite
apart from the fact that his father would now presumably be
unemployed. And on top of all this Barty himself came down
with typhoid. All things considered, it is not surprising that
going to university now became an insubstantial dream.

Mrs Barton was disappointed that her grandson never
matriculated and went to university – one of the events which
delighted her most in her later life was the decision of the

Senate, after many years of argument, to admit women. But it was clear that Barty would have to settle for an office desk of one kind or another. There had already been some talk of his becoming a solicitor, and now there was no alternative. In 1880, Barty left school, 'articles of agreement' were signed, and Mr A. B. Paterson entered the Sydney office of Spain and Salway, solicitors.

TWO

The Birth of 'The Banjo'

Paterson was happily the sort of man who would probably have settled down to any job, provided it interested him. Though he might not have chosen law as an occupation, (with him it could never really have been regarded as a profession), he found that from the start it at least brought him into contact with the everyday lives of a variety of people. These people came from classes and occupations of which he had no previous experience, and about whom he was endlessly curious.

Spain and Salway were predominantly solicitors who dealt with shipping matters, and one of the very first jobs he was given at sixteen, was to collect evidence on behalf of a captain prosecuted for not showing a riding-light over the stern of his boat while at anchor.

The case seemed water-tight: the captain swore that he had seen the boatswain put out the light, and the boatswain remembered placing it – he said he had almost fallen overboard while doing so. Paterson was stunned when having listened to them, the magistrate calmly found the captain guilty and fined him five pounds.

'I walked away from the court with the captain,' he later wrote, 'and was just starting to speak a piece about this awful iniquity when he said, "Oh, well – I didn't know you had to have a riding-light. They'd drive a man mad with their regulations in these bloody places." An unnerving experience.'[10]

The next five years were split, certainly in Paterson's mind, between existence at the office and his life outside it. While there is no evidence that he skimped on his work, he certainly never so much as hinted that he found it satisfactory. He was in time admitted as a solicitor, and his proud mother told his equally proud sister at home: 'Now remember, Barty's opinion is worth six and eightpence!', but he failed to discover a passion for the law. On the other hand, he certainly discovered a passion for social justice. In contrast to his life at Gladesville and the lives of the men and women he met at his grandmother's soirées, those to be seen in the back streets of Sydney were a very different matter.

He seems to have sought out adventures in those fascinating back streets, for he wrote of the life there in a political pamphlet which was his first published work. In it, he claims to have spent a night in 'one of the lower-class lodging houses in Sydney.' He had already been aghast at the 'wretched little shanties, the tiny stuffy rooms fairly reeking like ovens with the heat of our tropical summer', but the lodging house was even worse.

> I had 'roughed it' in the bush a great deal, I had camped out with little shelter and very little food. I had lived with the stockmen in their huts, on their fare, so I was not likely to be dainty, but after one night's experience in that lodging I dared not try a second. To the frightful discomfort was added the serious danger of disease from the filthy surroundings and the unhealthy atmosphere. I fled ... Do you, reader, believe that it is an inevitable law that in a wealthy country like this we must have so much poverty?

The drive of his first publication, *Australia for the Australians* (1889) was to argue against absentee landlords and for decentralisation, and he wrote with real intensity:

> It may be said that we are already the most prosperous country in the world; that in no other place can a good living be got so easily and certainly as it can here. Even if we grant this, it does not prove that we are as prosperous as we might be, or as we have every right to expect to be. And when we look into the matter we find that we are a very long

way from any such happy state. It ought to be possible in a new country like this for every man with a willing pair of hands to be always employed, and at good wages. There should be constant openings for our young men with brains and ability to make good incomes. Poverty and enforced idleness of willing men should be unknown. Yet we find the working men constantly seeking employment in vain. There seem to be less and less openings or chances for the young men who are coming forward ...

He strongly attacked those who owned land because their fathers or grandfathers had bought title to it, but failed to develop it:

The men who buy land in the early days of a settlement get a great deal of wealth to which they have no moral right. To illustrate what I mean, near Melbourne is a vast freehold estate owned by one family, and valued at a million of money. Almost all of this is in the same state as it was when Batman first settled on the place where Melbourne now is, as being a likely site for a village. It carries sheep and nothing else. From Williamstown right down nearly to Geelong you travel through it. Near Sydney, on the North Shore, is a vast unimproved block of water frontage property, which frowns on the harbour, bold and rugged, in just exactly the same state as it was when Captain Cook brought his ships round there. It is now worth hundreds of thousands of pounds. What has given these properties their value? Clearly not the labour and trouble of their owners, as they are unimproved ... To whom does the finest house about Sydney belong? It belongs to a man who inherited a huge fortune, made solely out of the rise and rents of real estate near Sydney; a man who counts his fortune by hundreds and thousands, and spends most of his time in England. He never did a day's work in his life, and yet can have every luxury, while thousands of his fellow countrymen have to toil and pinch and contrive to get a living. The more the country goes ahead the more he prospers, and the less he needs to do. It looks rather as if he 'had the loan of us', as the unrefined say. Yet it is not fair to blame the man. We should blame the rotten, absurd system which makes such a thing possible ...

He was even more impassioned when writing of the profiteers in the city itself:

When we hear of George Street property fetching a thousand pounds per foot, we say, 'How prosperous the country must be! What wonderful advances we are making! A few years ago it could have been bought for a hundred pounds an acre!' What we ought to say is, 'What a dreadful handicap on the colony it is, that men should be able to get such a lot of the colony's products for land which was increased in value by the State. What fools we are to allow it to go on!' That is what we ought to say. To anyone who understands the matter, it is a cruel thing to see the settlers in the interior of our colony striving day after day on their little properties, with no comforts, no leisure, no hopes nor aspirations beyond making a decent living, and to think it is all owing to the labour of these men and such as these that the owners of Sydney are living luxuriously, travelling between this

colony and England, drawing large rentals, or
spending large values which they never did a
hand's turn to earn or deserve.[11]

Paterson never wrote with quite such passion again about social
affairs and the pamphlet certainly shows that he had first-hand
experience of the large number of the poor living in what
was becoming a rich city. He always had a sympathy for the
underdog, though more for country than city people, and he
certainly knew the blacker areas of Sydney, and the men and
women who scraped a living there.

His 1889 pamphlet is the one piece of evidence
that he had an interest in social politics. He never became
a positive, consistent agitator for social reform, although he
was a passionate objector to the increasing employment of
Chinese workers in the country. These Chinese workers were
especially hated by the shearers, who often described them
as 'lepers' because of the popular belief that they carried this
disease, suggested by often scabby skin. (Incidentally, this is the
source of the term "scab" to describe non-union labour.) Later
Paterson ardently supported Prime Minister Edmund Barton's
1901 Immigration Act, and his argument that 'The doctrine of
the equality of man was never intended to apply to the equality
of the Englishman and the Chinaman.'

Much of Paterson's time was necessarily spent studying.
In August 1886 he sat a final examination and became officially,
an attorney and solicitor. He was a managing clerk for a while,
before going into partnership with John William Street, who
had for two years had a practice at 85 Pitt Street, Sydney. His
devotion to law, or certainly to work as a jobbing solicitor, was
never obsessive. Indeed he was highly critical of some aspects
of it such as the practise that even in negligible cases, solicitors
were not permitted to appear in court and counsel had to be
briefed, at considerable expense to impoverished plaintiffs. He
later satirised the practise in verse:

I am a barrister, wigged and gowned;
Of stately presence and look profound ...
I take your brief and I look to see
That the same is marked with a thumping fee;
But just as your case is drawing near
I bob serenely and disappear.
And away in another court I lurk
While a junior barrister does your work;
And I ask my fee with a courtly grace,
Although I never came near the case.
But the loss means ruin too you, maybe,
But nevertheless I must have my fee!
For the lawyer laughs in his cruel sport
While his clients march to the Bankrupt Court.[12]

Satire however, was neither Paterson's forte nor passion. Neither was political invective, but his first published verses, which appeared in *The Bulletin* in February 1885, were an impassioned attack on the sending of Australian troops to the Sudan to fight against the Mahdi, just after the fall of Khartoum and the death of General Gordon:

... fairest Australia freest of the free,
Is up in arms against the freeman's fight;
And with her mother joined to crush the right,
Has left her threatened treasures o'er the sea,
Has left her land of liberty and law
To flesh her maiden sword in this unholy war.

Enough! God never blessed such enterprise
England's degenerate Generals yet shall rue
Brave Gordon sacrificed, when soon they view
The children of a thousand deserts rise
To drive them forth like sand before the gate –
God and the Prophet! Freedom will prevail.[13]

The editor of *The Bulletin* paid Paterson seven shillings and sixpence, and encouraged him to contribute more verses. He found a little to his surprise, that it was easy enough to turn them out. On 30 October 1886 *The Bulletin* published 'A Dream of the Melbourne Cup':

> *Bring me a quart of colonial beer*
> *And some doughy damper to make good cheer,*
> *I must make a heavy dinner;*
> *Heavily dine and heavily sup,*
> *Of indigestible things fill up,*
> *Next month they run the Melbourne Cup,*
> *And I have to dream the winner ...*

He does so, and

> *A million to five is the price I get -*
> *Not bad! but before I book the bet*
> *The horse's name I clean forget,*
> *Its number and even gender ...*

> *I bet my coin on the Sydney crack,*
> *A million I've won, no question!*
> *'Give me my money, you hook-nosed hog!*
> *Give me my money, bookmaking dog!'*
> *But he disappeared in a kind of fog,*
> *And I woke with 'the indigestion'.*[14]

A couple of months later 'The Mylora Elopement' appeared: the first of the 'songs of the bush' which were to become the poet's speciality:

> *By the winding Wollondilly where the weeping*
> *   willows weep,*
> *And the shepherd, with his billy, half awake*
> *   and half asleep,*
> *Folds his fleecy flocks that linger homewards in*
> *   the setting sun*

> *Lived my hero, Jim the Ringer, 'cocky' on*
> *Mylora Run.*
> *Jimmy loved the super's daughter, Miss Amelia*
> *Jane McGrath.*
> *Long and earnestly he sought her, but he feared*
> *her stern papa;*
> *And Amelia loved him truly - but the course of*
> *love, if true,*
> *Never yet ran smooth or duly,*
> *as I think it ought to do ...*[15]

From that time Paterson 'versified' regularly in *The Bulletin*. Though he certainly wrote for profit, (and the profits were considerable after his verses appeared in book form), he clearly enjoyed celebrating and communicating in rhyme his passion for horses and the bush.

None of his colleagues or any of the men and women who consulted him professionally knew at first of his writing. From the very beginning he published under a pseudonym or with a set of initials: simply 'B.', or sometimes 'J. W.' Presumably he felt that to be known as a writer of light verse would be no assistance to his reputation as a solicitor. Not that all his verse was particularly light. He did from time to time use it as a fairly blunt weapon, as in 'A Bushman's Song':

> *I asked a cove for shearin' once along the*
> *Marthaguy:*
> *We shear non-union here', says he. 'I call it*
> *scab,' says I.*
> *I looked along the shearin' floor before I turned*
> *to go –*
> *There were eight or ten dashed Chinamen*
> *a-shearin' in a row.*
> *It was shift, boys, shift, for there wasn't the*
> *slightest doubt*
> *It was time to make a shift with the leprosy about,*
> *So I saddled up my horses, and I whistled to my dog,*
> *And I left his scabby station at the old jog-jog.*[16]

There is no mystery about where the pseudonym – 'The Banjo' – came from. He himself explained that it was originally the name of 'a so-called race-horse' which his family once owned. Over the years, of course, the secret got out, and the man who always remained Barty to his friends and family was known throughout Australia, and widely in England, as 'The Banjo'.[17]

Meanwhile, though his thoughts often strayed from the papers on his office desk to the open country he loved, he continued to make his living as a solicitor. It was barely a living. He managed to stay out of debt, but there was precious little money to spare after paying the rent of the rooms he shared with a colleague, and regular seven-and-sixpences from *The Bulletin* were extremely welcome. He also sold verses elsewhere – the *Sydney Mail* published the sentimental but highly effective *Lost*, which became one of his best-known verses.[18] He soon ceased his occasional contributions on professional subjects to *The Articled Clerks' Journal* as they were unpaid and extremely boring to write.

He clearly disliked some aspects of legal work such as chasing after debts and pursuing debtors who were clearly never going to be able to afford to re-pay. They were predestined to prison - a fate to which he could identify - just like being shut in an office for hours of the day and most of the days of the year when he had such a love of the open air:

> *... sitting in my dingy little office, where a*
> *stingy*
> *Ray of sunshine struggles feebly down between*
> *the houses tall,*
> *And the foetid air and gritty of the dusty, dirty city,*
> *Through the open window floating, spreads its*
> *foulness over all ...*[19]

Happily, sometimes office work brought a sudden flash of inspiration or indeed the simple gift of a memorable line or two. One time having written a standard letter to a debtor, he received the scribbled answer: 'Clancy's gone to Queensland droving and we don't know where he are', a line which later became the hub of *Clancy of the Overflow*,[20] which *The Bulletin* published in December 1889. The Banjo's best-known ballad:, *The Man from Snowy River,* was published four months later and the stockman at the centre of it has also often been claimed as a real person (a fact even recorded on his tombstone!).

The Banjo put a stop to such stories in an article in the *Sydney Mail* almost fifty years later: 'To make any sort of job of [the ballad],' he wrote, 'I had to create a character, to imagine a man who could ride better than anyone else. And what sort of horse would he ride except a half-thoroughbred mountain pony? ...' There had certainly really been a 'Man from Snowy River' – but 'more than one of them'.[21]

With a slowly increasing income from his professional world, and subsidy from his contributions to *The Bulletin* and other papers, Paterson gradually began to make his way with a greater belief in achieving eventual security, if not prosperity. One result of this was his engagement to Sarah Ann Riley, an acquaintance of his partner, John Street. He seems to have proposed to her in 1888, when he was 24 and she was 25 – though they probably knew each other for some years before that. The courtship does not appear to have been a passionate one, to say the least, nor particularly enthusiastic. After the engagement had lasted seven years, Sarah broke it off and neither party seemed to particularly regret the fact.

There is little evidence of the kind of relationship that existed between the two, but there is little doubt that during their engagement, Paterson was living more and more in his own world – at least when the ties of his profession did not chain him to his office desk. He had moved to a flat of his own in Bond Street and made it a sort of shrine to the bush. But as Colin Roderick pointed out in his 1993 biography, *Banjo: poet by accident* [22] he had never actually been near the real outback - the great brown country existed only in his imagination.

In the meantime he got to know Henry Lawson, another contributor to The Bulletin. Lawson's upbringing was not more fortunate than Paterson's. Born on the Grenfell goldfields of New South Wales, his father (originally Niels Herzberg Larsen, from Norway, who later anglicised his name) was a miner, his mother Louisa Lawson a suffragette who played a considerable part in the fight for women's suffrage. Henry went to school at Eurunderee, now a suburb of Mudgee, but contracted an ear infection which made him completely deaf by the time he was fourteen.

At a later school he was encouraged by a sympathetic master and became an inveterate reader and writer. While working as a labourer, he began submitting verse to The Bulletin and had his first contribution: *A Song of the Republic*, published in its columns in 1887. He was an enthusiastic republican and a great deal further to the left, politically, than The Banjo. He had more literary experience too, for he spent time in Brisbane editing *Boomerang*, a republican magazine which soon failed.

Lawson and Paterson were soon perceived as rivals in the columns of *The Bulletin*. They had one thing in common: though he versified enthusiastically on the subject, Lawson had never been any nearer to the real bush than The Banjo, who wrote of him that he 'was a man of remarkable insight in some things and of extraordinary simplicity in others. We were both looking for the same reef, if you get what I mean; but I had done my prospecting on horseback with my meals cooked for me, while Lawson had done his prospecting on foot and had had to cook for himself. Nobody realised this better than Lawson, and one day he suggested that we should write against each other, he putting the bush from his point of view, and I putting it from mine. 'We ought to do pretty well out of it,' he said, 'we ought to be able to get in three or four sets of verses before they stop us.'[23]

So, already seen as rivals by readers of *The Bulletin*, they engaged in a poetic battle on the subject of bush life. Lawson began with a set of verses entitled 'Borderland', in which he described the outback with treacherous tracks that led the stranger astray, 'dark and evil-looking gullies' and 'dull dumb flats'. It was a place where one encountered 'the sinister "gohanna" and the lizard and the snake', where the men were always away from home trying to make money while 'gaunt and haggard women live alone and work like men.'

The Banjo replied with some lyrical lines about 'the silver chiming of the bell-birds on the range', but mainly attacked Lawson as a 'townee':

*No doubt you're better suited drinking lemon
   squash in town,
You had better stick to Sydney and make merry
   with the 'push',
For the bush will never suit you, and you'll
   never suit the bush.*[24]

'We slam-banged away at each other for weeks and weeks,' he remembered; 'not until they stopped us, but until we ran out of material'. What he and Lawson hadn't reckoned on was that a number of other versifiers would join in the debate – including one regular contributor, Edward Dyson, and a number of others, some simply writing their initials, some signing themselves in full. But it was Paterson and Lawson who were the main combatants and who got the publicity they sought. If the impression was given that they were bitter rivals who scorned each other's views and abilities, this is far from the truth. 'I think that Lawson put his case better than I did, but I had the better case, so that honours (or dishonours) were fairly equal,' wrote Paterson years later, remembering the escapade as 'an undignified affair'.

In the end, if Lawson won the 'battle in rhyme', it was probably The Banjo, in his melancholy poem 'Under the Shadow of Kiley's Hill', who most memorably acknowledged the hardship of bush life:

*Where are the children that strove and grew
In the old homestead in days gone by?
One is away on the far Barcoo
Watching his cattle the long year through,
Watching them starve in the droughts and die.*

*One, in the town where all cares are rife,
Weary with troubles that cramp and kill,
Fain would be done with the restless strife,*

Fain would go back to the old bush life,
Back to the shadow of Kiley's Hill.

One is away on the roving quest,
Seeking his share of the golden spoil;
Out in the wastes of the trackless west,
Wandering ever he gives the best
Of his years and strength to the hopeless toil.

While for the rest of his life he professed a love of the bush and of bush life, and to some extent continued to glamorise it, he was always conscious of the suffering which too often lay behind the romantic veneer he threw over it in some of his ballads.

Over a century later, it seems to a modern reader almost incredible that readers of a daily newspaper should pick up an issue looking eagerly for one poet's versified response to the verses of another – indeed almost incredible that a newspaper should publish poetry at all. But it was common practise for many editors of the period both in Australia and England. In Sydney, apart from Paterson and Lawson there were Barcroft Boake, Will Ogilvie, A. L. Gordon, E. J. Brady and Edward Dyson. The latter were equally as popular as the first two, so that they were known at one time as 'Paterdylaw and Son'. They were all bush-ballad writers, all celebrating Australia and a way of life they saw as illustrating the basic identity of Australians. There was also Breaker Morant.

Morant was probably first introduced to Paterson by his uncle, Arthur Sterling Barton, although The Banjo may first have run into Morant at *The Bulletin* offices, for between 1891 and 1901 Morant published over sixty poems in that paper. Barton certainly wrote to Paterson about Morant, telling him that he was the son of an English Admiral, had had a good English education, and apart from writing verses could break in horses (hence his nickname), 'trap dingoes, yard scrub cattle, dance, run, fight, drink and borrow money; anything except work.' Apart from that he was a magnificent horseman, said to have once jumped a horse over a three-rail fence on a moonless night, guided only by the flickering light of two matches he had placed on the posts.

No doubt it was Morant's reputation as a horseman that attracted Paterson, mad on horses as they both were. It is doubtful whether The Banjo would have been any less friendly to Morant even had he known that The Breaker was actually the son of the master and matron of a workhouse in Somerset, whose real name was Murrant. (He had assumed the more aristocratic-sounding name of Henry Harbord Morant when writing a bad cheque in payment for some horses a year after arriving in Australia in 1883).

There are various accounts (none of them reliable), of where and when the two men first met. What is clear is that The Breaker and The Banjo hit it off immediately and a wary mutual respect kept them friends. At their first meeting Morant asked Paterson to change a cheque for him, and Paterson refused, so they both knew where they stood. The great tie between them of course was their mutual passion for horses and riding – Paterson did not share Morant's almost equally passionate addiction to alcohol. Both passions are addressed in an undated letter from Morant:

> When I came over here the other day, it was to participate in a hurrah spree to finish the bachelor days of the manager here. He is about to take unto himself a wife of his own! Most fellows up here generally get shook on, or content with, some other fellow's spouse. Anyhow, I was unsteadily tripping across to my bedroom in the small, murky hours of the morning, and went headlong down some 18ft. of a cellar. Left shoulder dislocated was the result. An amateur surgeon pulled it in again without chloroform next morning, but a ten days complete rest mostly camping under the flow of an artesian bore, and frequent applications of arnica have put me pretty right once more ...

I have done a bit of brumby running in mountain country, although most of my cleanskin experience has been in mulga or brigalow, and I have noticed that a good man on a plucky horse can always beat brumbies when going down a declivity. A horse with a rider on his back goes with confidence, whilst brumbies are never all out then. When going uphill the naked horse gets away. Weight tells then, I suppose, though of course there is the chance of a smash going down.'[25]

In the end, everything came round to horses. Apart from that interest, they clearly shared an enthusiasm for 'field sports', exchanging enthusiastic anecdotes about dog-fighting, bare-fist fighting, pig-sticking, stag-hunting and the excitement of ripping wild cattle open with a knife while riding alongside them. From the start Paterson recognised Morant for the chancer he was - one of his poems seems to start out as a portrait of The Breaker:

> Born of a thoroughbred English race,
> Well proportioned and closely knit,
> Neat, slim figure and handsome face,
> Always ready and always fit,
> Hardy and wiry of limb and thew,
> That was the ne'er-do-well Jim Carew ...
>
> Gentleman Jim in the stockmen's hut
> Works with them, toils with them, side by side;
> As to his past - well, his lips are shut.
> 'Gentleman once,' say his mates with pride,
> And the wildest Cornstalk can ne'er outdo
> In feats of recklessness Jim Carew.[26]

The poem ends with Carew as a wreck, ruined by drink and duplicity; maybe Paterson saw this as the probable result of the life Morant was leading. He was mistaken: a different fate awaited The Breaker.

Meanwhile there was fun to be had and Paterson enjoyed Morant's cavalier way of courting danger and smartly recovering from its effects. On one occasion he had a bad fall at steeplechasing and was carried off the course unconscious. 'All the bystanders thought he was in a bad way. They plied him with questions, but could get no satisfaction from him till someone asked in a loud, clear voice, "What will you have, Morant?" He at once replied, "Brandy and soda", and his recovery was marvellously rapid.'[27]

Paterson and Morant shared a love of polo – once The Banjo came across the sport, very new to Australia, it was inevitable given his passion for riding that it should be one that claimed all his enthusiasm. 'When a cavalry officer came out from England and started a polo club we took to the game like ducks to water', he later said. 'The polo business brought us in touch with the upper circles – a great change after the little bush school, the game-cocks, and the days when I looked upon the sergeant of police as the greatest man in the world.'[28] No doubt many a bad cheque found its way from the chequebook of The Breaker into the wallet of some naïve English subaltern.

However not all their games were with the great and good. Paterson based his poem 'The Geebung Polo Club'[29] on a match played against a team from Cooma, a little town settled in 1823 at the centre of the Monaro grazing area. They were 'real wild men with cabbage-tree hats and skin-tight pants, their hats held on by a strap under their noses'. But he more often played in formal games, for instance as a member of the team which won the New South Wales polo championship in 1892. His work as a solicitor and as a writer, whether in verse or prose, took second place to his overwhelming passion for horses. But it was his writing which was to make his name a household word in Australia and elsewhere.

THREE

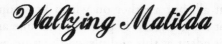

Waltzing Matilda

The verses signed 'The Banjo', appearing regularly in *The Bulletin*, had attracted the attention of a young Sydney businessman. George Robertson was born in England, where he started his working life apprenticed to a publisher. Arriving in Sydney in 1882, he naturally looked to the world of books for employment. He began work at a second-hand bookshop in Market Street Sydney, which had been established eighteen months earlier by David Angus. The two men eventually went into partnership and Angus and Robertson did well from the start. They soon moved into offices in Castlereagh Street and began to publish in a small way. Their first book was a collection of verse, A *crown of wattle*, by Sydney solicitor H. Peden Steel. In 1894 Robertson approached Paterson with a view to publishing a collection of his poems, even though he was extremely critical of Paterson's work and did not believe there were enough first-rate poems for a book yet. He asked if The Banjo could supply some more.

Paterson said he would think about it and meanwhile decided to take a short holiday from Sydney. He travelled north to Queensland with his *fiancée* of eight years, Sarah Riley, who had been invited to stay with her brother, Frederick Whistler Riley, at Winton. Winton was 170 kilometres from the end of the railway line at Rockhampton (nowadays some seventeen hours' drive from Brisbane). Frederick and his wife lived in 'Aloha', a bungalow in Vindex Street, where Paterson and Sarah stayed during March and April of 1895.

It was here they met an old school friend of Sarah's, Christina Macpherson, who was on holiday with her sister Jean and their father Ewan. Ewan's brother Robert was at Dagworth station on the Diamantina River, 130 kilometres north of Winton. The family went up to Dagworth for a visit, and it seems that at some stage they settled down for a sing-song. Christina, or so the story goes, had recently been to a race meeting at Warrnambool in Victoria, and there had heard a band playing a tune which had stuck in her mind. There was no piano at Dagwood, but they had an autoharp – really not a harp at all, but a zither on which keys suppress all the strings except those chosen to give out the tune and harmony. Christina was adept at this and played the tune, which proved catchy enough to stick in The Banjo's head.

Precisely how the words of 'Waltzing Matilda' were matched to the tune, and what inspired those words, is a subject over which there has been much debate. So much so, that if there were indeed ever any facts about the matter, they have long been obscured. No doubt some of the local stories[30] stuck like the tune in Paterson's mind, to emerge in an obscure way in the verses. Whether specifically written or not, they roughly matched the catchy tune. At all events, Christina strummed out on the autoharp the verses on the autoharp and they proved an instant success – and not only with the family. Within a matter of days, they were being enthusiastically sung in Winton pubs.

The song failed to travel south with The Banjo when he returned home to Sydney, and he sold the verses to Angus and Robertson for five pounds. They in turn sold the copyright at a profit of five shillings, to the firm of Inglis & Co, tea merchants, who used it to publicise their 'Billy' brand of tea. The original lines scribbled down by Paterson at Dagworth could barely be made to fit the tune, so the wife of Inglis' manager slightly edited them, and the song was published as it is sung today. Paterson was clearly completely unaware of the potential value of what he had created – and why would he not be? 'Waltzing Matilda' was after all a mere skit compared with his ballads. Indeed it was some time before it became widely popular - between the two world wars.

From time to time over the past century several harebrained theories have been put forward explaining that Paterson was not the author of the verses. These include that he had no idea what a 'Matilda' was, that he made a fortune from the song, that he made nothing at all from the song, that the music was written by this composer or that. The truth is too simple to satisfy some people: that the tune stuck sufficiently in Paterson's head to provide him with the rhythm of the verses.;

That the lines emerged in the way lines do emerge, obscurely and often effortlessly, from a writer's mind; that married together, the words and music have that memorable quality which the most popular folk songs have – they have become so much a part of Australia's character that they forever represent it to a listener.

Though it is best to avoid applying to 'Waltzing Matilda' the kind of literary analysis which devotes pages of scrutiny to every line, it seems obvious that one of the early appeals of the song was to those Australians who thoroughly approved of a swagman collaring the occasional sheep. It also appealed to those who were less than happy with the squatters who grabbed land illegally, made fortunes when given tenure by the land acts of the 1860s, and were hard on the swagmen who usually had less than nothing. The Banjo certainly shared that view despite his legal training, and if he did not positively intend his verses as social criticism, that in the end is what they were, and are. For what other reason would a nation take to its heart a poem about theft and suicide?

Winton and Dagworth both happily represent themselves as the places where 'Waltzing Matilda' was born. But neither place in the end held happy memories for Paterson. During his holiday there, his engagement to Sarah Riley came to an end. It was perhaps time – after all, it had been much longer than common. Given the fact that he was now reasonably financially secure, there was no excuse for further delay - Sarah was now 32 and time was going on. She probably simply lost patience and decided that enough was enough – though stories also surfaced suggesting that Paterson had been flirting with Christina, and that Sarah took exception to it. At all accounts the engagement, which never seems to have been particularly enthusiastic, let alone passionate, came to a sudden end. Sarah left Australia for England and The Banjo returned to Sydney alone. Within six months, stories were current inside and outside his family that that he was putting himself about fairly vigorously among the young women of the town, including a prominent and beautiful *divorcée*. It was even suggested that he was engaged to several of them – most notably a Miss Alice

Cape, a young Roman Catholic girl. He was also seen escorting his beautiful cousin Dorothea, who had just left school, and there was more talk. Paterson kept his counsel.

Apart from flirtation, there was the business of the proposed collection of poems. Robertson kept agitating for more. The Banjo put his mind to the task, and though he sent Robertson some verses which he had written previously but had not yet published, he also turned out an astonishing number of new ones. Robertson sent some of them back – not good enough - and again demanded more. Paterson obliged and among the last he submitted - a batch of eight - were some of his best, including 'Under the Shadow of Kiley's Hill' and 'Brumby's Run'.[31]

The Man from Snowy River and Other Verses came out in October 1895 and a second edition was ordered even before the publication of the first. One of the reasons for the success of Angus and Robertson was George Robertson's attention to detail. In the days before publishers had publicity departments, he personally sent out a great number of review copies to newspapers both in England and America, and to all the major Australian booksellers. They were impressed, and ordered over two thousand copies of the book before publication. Within two months over three thousand copies had been sold, and the reviews were uniformly enthusiastic. What probably pleased Paterson most was a letter from one of the best-known living English poets, Rudyard Kipling, in which he sent his 'best salutations', and encouraged Paterson to 'do it again' – to 'write more and more about the man who is born and bred on the land.'

By April 1896 five thousand copies of *The Man from Snowy River* had been sold in Australia and New Zealand, another thousand was being printed, and an edition of a thousand had been sent off to England. Reviews were equally enthusiastic there: *The Times* compared The Banjo with Kipling and the book did much to bring the English their first glimpse of bush life. An anonymous critic wrote in *The Spectator* that the poems 'take hold of the mind from the passionate love they express of the Australian scenery and from the stimulating character of the wild and lonely life of the station or the drover on those silent hills and plains.' The *Glasgow Herald* found the ballads 'so full of go that the mere reading makes the blood tingle'.

Within a very few months the best of The Banjo's ballads were being read – and recited – across the whole of literate Australia. The time, the age, was of course right for them. Without any other means of entertainment than reading and home-made music, it would have been difficult for the book to fail. If today the best of the verses still convey the exhilaration of the wide open air, of the spirit of early Australia, it is not surprising that when they were newly-minted there was scarcely a dissenting voice among the chorus of praise for them.

The Banjo was now pretty much written-out and he published very little verse during 1896. Perhaps slightly oppressed by his celebrity and the chores of being a kind of public figure, he spent the following two years away from Sydney. He went first to his cousins in Queensland, seeking out bush songs much as Percy Grainger, years later, was to seek out folk songs in Britain. Then in 1898, travelling around the Northern Territory, he was asked by the South Australian Government to write something which would attract tourists to excursions organized by the Eastern and Australian Steamships Company.

The result was an article which was reprinted in *The Bulletin* at Christmas 1898, in which Paterson was less than enthusiastic about the Territory's prospects:

> To sum up, the Northern Territory is a vast, wild land, full of high possibilities, but, up to now, a colossal failure. She has leagues and leagues of magnificent country – with no water. Miles and miles of splendidly watered country – where the grass is sour, rank, and worthless. Mines with rich ore – that it doesn't pay to treat. Quantities of precious stones – that have no value. The pastoral industry and the mines are not paying, and the pearling, which does, is getting too much into Jap hands. The hordes of aliens that

have accumulated are a menace to the rest of Australia ...'[32]

Returning to Sydney, The Banjo found the idea of settling down to his legal practise repulsive to the point of nausea. He had never enjoyed confinement to an office, and his travels had made it even more difficult to consider tolerating it. Instead, he went to the editor of the *Sydney Morning Herald* and offered his services as a special correspondent reporting the Boer War. He yearned for the open air and for excitement, and the war would no doubt provide both, one way or another. It is entirely possible that if he had been able-bodied, he would even have enlisted as a soldier. He sailed from Sydney for South Africa on 30 October 1899 – less than three weeks after the declaration of war.

FOUR

The Banjo at War

The conflict was between the overwhelming forces of Britain, fielding at the height of the war almost half a million men, and the 88,000 or so men fighting for two Boer or Afrikaner republics, the Transvaal or South African Republic and the Orange Free State. The war had started on 11 October, after the President of the Republic, Paul Kruger, had refused to grant political rights to the Uitlanders or foreigners working in the mining areas of Witwatersrand. This gave enormous offence to the British High Commissioner, Viscount Milner, and the British Colonial Secretary, Joseph Chamberlain, who took action not so much because of the denial of suffrage to British subjects but due to their country's lack of control of the gold-mining industry of the Transvaal, the largest in the world, at a time when Britain badly needed gold.

This trio of Kruger, Milner and Chamberlain was obdurate in the extreme - no-one was going to give way. Milner in particular was immovable, as Paterson was to write, 'He has a lot on his shoulders, as he conducted all the negotiations with Kruger. If any one man is responsible for the war, then Milner is the man.'

Initially, the Boers were taking advantage of British weakness and lack of preparation by moving into Natal from the Transvaal and the northern Cape from the Orange Free State while the men of the northern districts of the Cape Colony were rebelling against the British and joining Boer forces. Meanwhile, Banjo Paterson was spending his last days in Sydney stalling his horses and settling into his quarters on the transport ship *Kent,* in company with thirty-eight lancers and ninety-one officers and men of the medical corps. He took two horses with him - a thoroughbred gelding which he was used to riding, and a smaller beast given to him by a friend. The other horses on board were mainly police horses, seconded to South African duties by the Government.

The *Kent* was cheered out of harbour by all the vessels in port – and by a steamer-load of newsboys who had chartered a boat especially to see her off. There was chaos on the *Kent* from the word go, when the army medical men came on board a day earlier than anyone else, confiscated generous quarters and barricaded themselves in, closing the doors to other parts of the ship. They also commandeered all the hammocks they could lay their hands on, and sat tight. The lancers were furious, and the relationship between them and the medical men barely avoided physical conflict. But if the lancers had to put up with congested, uncomfortable quarters, the horses had a worse time of it. The deck beneath their hooves became slippery, and even in a mild swell they slid backwards and forwards in their stalls, at one moment with their forefeet braced out in front of them, the next falling back on their haunches. When the *Kent* ran into stormy weather in the Bight they rattled around in their stalls often unable to keep their feet. They were to suffer even more during the long, rolling swell on the voyage from King George Sound to Port Elizabeth, in South Africa. As Paterson scribbled, later:

> When you're lying in your hammock, sleeping
>   soft and sleeping sound,
> Without a care or trouble on your mind,
> And there's nothing to disturb you but the
>   engines going round,
> And you're dreaming of the girl you left behind;
> In the middle of your joys you'll be wakened by
>   a noise
> And a clatter on the deck above your crown,
> And you'll hear the corporal shout as he turns
>   the picket out,
> 'There's another bloody horse fell down.'
>
> You can see em in the morning, when you're
>   cleaning out the stall,
> A-leaning on the railings nearly dead,

And you reckon by the evening they'll be pretty
sure to fall;
And you curse them as you tumble into bed.
Oh, you'll hear it pretty soon, 'Pass the word for
Denny Moon,
There's a horse here throwing handsprings like a
clown;'
And it's shove the others back, or he'll cripple
half the pack;
'There's another bloody horse fell down.' [33]

The Banjo grumbled that while the men got a bottle of beer every day for dinner and half a tin of salmon each at every meal, no-one had thought of the comfort of the horses. Even without rough weather, the stalls, which had been ill-fitted, often almost carried away – which would have resulted in those horses stupidly stalled on a hatch three feet above the deck plunging down onto the ones below. It was surprising that only one animal was lost during the entire voyage. He did however show a touch of that humour with which he was always able to lighten the grimmest of his dispatches: Col. W. D. C. Williams, in command of the medical forces, was giving his men rifle practise, shooting at a box towed behind the ship, and revolver practise with bottles thrown over the side as targets. 'No-one has yet sunk a bottle,' Paterson reported, 'and some of the shooters have even missed the Indian Ocean.[34]

Paterson started his record of the war no more sensitively than any other correspondent who saw it as part of his duty to whip up prejudice against the enemy. He reported a conversation with an ambulance orderly who asserted that the Boers not only fired on ambulances but on the cavalry. (With his love of horses, just the kind of statement to wind him up.) 'By all accounts the Boers,' he concluded, 'are only partly human.'[35] Later, he met a Boer prisoner-of-war, a doctor with a degree from an English university, who commanded Paterson's respect because he could make a fifty break at billiards: 'Apparently these Boers are at any rate partially civilized', he conceded.

The Australian contingent arrived at Port Elizabeth (the arid coast of South Africa looked like Bondi without the houses), where they found men from the Welsh Fusiliers, Brabant's Horse and the Prince Alfred Guard already stationed. 30,000 more men were expected shortly from Britain. When the pilot came on board, Paterson asked if he thought 180 horses could be safely landed. The man replied tersely that a thousand mules had been landed without any difficulty, a couple of days earlier. The Mayor then came on board and gave an address of welcome, champagne was opened, and a chorus of 'God Save the Queen' was sung before the *Kent* weighed anchor and sailed on to Cape Town, docking there, amid a flurry of other transport ships. From the deck they saw on land, lines of white tents where troops from Victoria were camped.

Somehow Paterson stole a march on several other correspondents by managing to interview the Cape Town High Commissioner, Sir Alfred Milner, even before leaving the *Kent*. Why the Commissioner came on board is a mystery – had he perhaps read *The Man from Snowy River*? Milner was 'a long, dark, wiry man, with a somewhat high-strung temperament; but he has been a pressman, so nothing ought to rattle him ... Hitherto, the only English magnates I have met have been State governors - discreet personages, whose official view of life could be summed up in three words: "I'd better not." But this man has actually used the words "You must", and has stood to his guns...' Later Paterson commented: 'He had some job, had Sir Alfred Milner, as the German Emperor was sending messages of congratulation to Kruger, and the American Press were roasting the war for all they were worth. Milner was my first experience of the unhurried Englishman. I met the "jumpy" sort later on. But the jumpy sort never get into those big jobs ...'[36]

In short he liked Milner, and Milner seems to have taken to him. When said he wanted to accompany the Australian troops to the front, Milner laughed and said that soon there would be more correspondents at the front than fighting men – but promised to send a note to the Chief Press Censor advising that the Australians should have their own reporter with them.

Meanwhile the horses were disembarked, surprisingly spry after their voyage: 'Not one of them showed the slightest signs of wear and tear from the trip. They were very terrified at landing, the long spell at sea having apparently frightened them for all other purposes. The first that was landed promptly kicked a trooper, but without doing any harm. They were led about and had a roll, and a saddle was tried on one or two, and lo and behold before the day was out they were all doing slow exercise without seeming particularly stiff. They looked light and wiry alongside the English horses, but the authorities here pronounce them the finest lot of horses yet landed.'[37]

While The Banjo was hanging about waiting for the opportunity to move up with the troops, Milner invited, or rather commanded him to a jackal hunt in company with two titled Englishwomen, the Duchess of Westminster and Lady Charles Bentinck. Rather surprisingly, Paterson seems to have been quite eager to fraternise with the aristocracy – perhaps because 'both were young and attractive women, beautifully turned out, and their features had all the repose that marks the caste of Vere de Vere.' The ladies carried generous flasks of whisky and water and smoked incessantly, 'accomplishments which had not, at that time, penetrated to the lower orders' Paterson ironically observed. They showed no signs of being concerned at being placed in the hands of an unknown Australian, 'in fact I don't think anything on earth could have rattled them. When you are a duchess, you let other people do the worrying.' He realised that 'they looked upon me as the Wild Colonial Boy, the bronco buster from the Barcoo, and I determined to act up to it. It seemed a pity to disappoint them.' So when Lady Bentinck supposed that he rode a hundred miles a day in Australia, he 'told them that if I had a horse in Australia that wouldn't carry me a hundred miles a day. I would give him to a Chinaman to draw a vegetable cart. That appeared to be the stuff to give em.'

There was relatively little conversation. Paterson asked whether ladies rode astride in England, and the Duchess said no, they didn't, because it would give the horses sore backs. Flabbergasted, Paterson desisted, and silence ensued until the ladies began to talk between themselves about various members of the British high command. 'They should never have sent him out, my dear. Goodness knows how old he is, and he rouges and wears stays. No wonder he walked his men right straight into a Boer camp, instead of going where he was told. But, of course, he's a great friend of the Prince of Wales...' From the ladies, and later from his British fellow correspondents, Paterson got the indelible impression that 'everything in England was run by aristocratic cliques, each clique being headed by some duchess or other.'

The jackal hunt itself went reasonably well, and the ladies sat and smoked while a Dutch farmer dug the animal out, using a vast array of English obscenities, the meaning of which he appeared to be ignorant.[38]

The Banjo was less than impressed by the red tape and bungling he saw around him in Cape Town, and by the attitude of some British officers to the Australian contingent. He wrote for *The Bulletin* a sketch in which he depicted a scene at British HQ with a hard-pressed, elderly clerk trying to cope with messages from hither and yon. A clerk rushes in with a telegram from Tasmania:

> 'They offer to send a Commander-in-Chief and eighty-five men.'
> 'Well I am damned! Eighty-five men! You cable back and say that I've seen bigger armies on the stage at Drury Lane Theatre. Just wire and say this isn't a pantomime. They haven't got to march round and round a piece of scenery. Tell em to stop at home and breed!' ...
> 'They want to know, if they pay the men's fares over, will the British Government pay their return fares?'
> 'Yes! I should think we would. We'll put em in the front and there won't be so many of 'em to go back. If the colonies had any sense they'd have paid the return fares.'

And later, the beleaguered officer's back is broken by the final straw: two circus-owners in Sydney have promised six circus horses.

> 'Six circus horses! ... Perhaps they could let us have a few sword-swallowers to get off with the Boers' weapons? Look here, now – hand the whole thing over to one of the senior clerks, and tell him to do exactly what he damn well pleases in the matter, but that if he comes in here to ask any questions about it, I'll have him shot! Now go and don't you come here any more or I'll have you shot too! Take this cheque for a hundred thousand to the petty-cash department, and tell that contractor outside that his tender is two millions over the estimate, and don't let me hear any more of this blessed Australian army.'[39]

Not the first war correspondent to despair of certain aspects of the way the war was being run in so-called command posts well behind the lines, The Banjo made more than one satirical attack on perceived inefficiency. While this no doubt made him unpopular in some quarters, in others he was seen to be well on the side of the fighting men. Milner was as good as his word and the Press Censor accredited him as a war correspondent assigned to the New South Wales Lancers. He travelled over 500 kilometres with them by train to join General Sir John French's cavalry division defending Naauwpoort against Boer attack.

Naauwpoort was, he said, 'a dreadful place' – just a lot of small galvanised iron houses and a dust storm so thick that whole mule wagons sometimes drove into each other in the dust, not being able to see a yard ahead. If Paterson had suspected that he would at some time be likely to face danger, this was the time when the fact was confirmed. He came under fire for the first time and very soon concluded that he didn't care for it. In and around the British camps in the neighbourhood, seven of his fellow correspondents were killed or injured. The representative of the Melbourne *Age* was shot and killed at Jasfontein while riding with a patrol, and in the same incident, the correspondent of the London *Daily News* was thrown from his horse and made prisoner, spending the following four months in a prisoner-of-war camp in Pretoria.

Though conscious of danger, The Banjo ignored it, spending almost every hour of every day on horseback moving from camp to camp – Arundel to Rensburg to Slingersfortein – often carrying dispatches through wild country infinitely more familiar to the sniping Boer sharp-shooters than to him. That he survived must be more a tribute to luck than discretion. He rapidly won a reputation for being first with the news – which meant not only learning the facts but getting them back to Sydney as quickly as possible. He once woke the Chief Censor, Lord Derby, at 3 a.m. to vet a dispatch.

He soon recognised the fighting strategy over the plains and hills - the veldt and the kopjes – around Naauwpoort. 'No better fighting ground for cavalry could be found than the veldt,' he wrote, 'and no worse ground could be found than the kopje. A kopje in full working order is as good a fortress as can be imagined – a great heap of loose stones, with a little covering of sage-like brushwood. No horse in the world could get up it, and the most daring infantry would hesitate to attack it.' The fighting was as dangerous as it was fierce, and conditions had nothing to do with any romantic ideas that readers at home in Sydney might have of the noble calling of soldiering. It was not, Paterson wrote, an amusement: 'Out all day in the sun, up all night on watch, hungry, sunburnt, thirsty and unspeakably dirty, there is no glory about it. Our Lancers are hung all over with weapons and gear like a Christmas tree. Each man has a lance, sword, rifle and revolver. They will stand a good chance of getting killed before they can make up their minds which weapon to use.'[40]

During a pause in the action, the Lancers transferred from Naauwpoort to Randam in the Orange Free State, where the newly arrived Lord Roberts, taking over command with Lord Kitchener as his Chief of Staff, was assembling forces for an assault on the capital, Bloemfontein. Meanwhile, Paterson returned to Cape Town to conduct an interview with Olive Schreiner, the sister of the Prime Minister of the Cape Colony. She was an author, an extremely intelligent and forceful woman, and determined that he should understand the Boer side of the argument.

'You Australians and New Zealanders and Canadians', she said, 'I cannot understand it at all, why you come here lightheartedly to shoot down other colonists of whom you know nothing – it is terrible ... I saw your men in camp; oh, they were fine men, and to think they are going out to kill and be killed, just to please the capitalists! ... You ought to make enquiries before you come over. You Australians do not understand. This is a capitalists' war! They want to get control of the Rand and the mines. You have nothing like it in your country. You have a working class that votes and that cannot be brought to vote against its own interests; but in the Transvaal there are just a handful of Boer farmers, a small but enormously wealthy mine-owning class and their dependents – professional men, shop-keepers and so on, and the rest are all Kaffirs.[41]

She was completely convinced that the Boers would never capitulate and Paterson, persuaded, thought and wrote that this meant that 'England has a sorry task before her. If the Boers scatter and break to the mountains they will be practically unreachable, and the English people are too humane to care about levying reprisals by destroying their homesteads and leaving their wives and children without shelter.'[42]

By the time the British, largely on Kitchener's orders, were doing just that, and moreover putting women and children into concentration camps and using them as hostages, Paterson was back on a lecture circuit in Australia. But though he disagreed entirely with Olive Schreiner's point of view, and condescendingly suggested that instead of meddling in politics she should stick to her writing, he publicly agreed with her that the war would not be the walk-over that some folk thought.

During the following month Paterson was preoccupied with the campaign for the relief of Kimberley. Field Marshal Lord Roberts had instructed General John French to attempt this, and successfully crossing the Modder River, French ordered his forces to charge up the valley, forcing their way through the Boer lines and on to Kimberley. Paterson watched from a hilltop, as a force of 15,000 mounted men moved forward spreading over the plain below. As the regiments moved forward 'it was the grandest sight any of us ever hoped to see ... A confused sound rose from the vast mass, made by the horses' hoofs, the roll of the gun wheels, and the rattle of the lances.'

The road to Kimberley open, the Boer forces seemed to be taken completely by surprise: 'they left their coffee half-drunk, their meals half-eaten, and their tents standing, and fled.' It had been an astonishing gamble on French's part – and a brilliant one, but though he lost only one man dead and twenty wounded, the damage to the horses was high – which naturally attracted Paterson's attention. The day after the relief, he went around the town and looked at the wreckage:

> Horses that have collapsed through heat and overwork are being shot in all directions. The people here have been living on horseflesh and thousands of starving Kaffirs are hanging round the lines. When a horse is shot, they fling themselves on it like a crowd of vultures, and in ten minutes there is not a scrap left.[43]

The overladen Australian police horses had suffered particularly – they were smaller than the English cavalry horses, which could bear weights of seventeen or eighteen stone, while the Australian horses buckled under more than six or seven. Their food was also insufficient – a handful of corn first thing, then some raw oats at midday as they stood still heavily burdened and often left saddled for two days or more under the blazing sun. The Banjo justly complained:

> It would have taken a lot of iron horses to stand the vicious mishandling to which the poor four-footed servants of the Army were subjected. Good horse, or bad horse, right

type, or wrong type, the ill-treatment and
hardships they had to undergo brought them
all to one level, and the 'five-pound scrubber'
was quite as likely to survive as the finest
specimen of the weight carrying charger. It
was not the severity of the work they had to
do which killed them; but it was the wretched
conditions under which they did their work.
If our horses could have been kept free from
sickness, and have been properly fed, they
could have done all the Army work with the
greatest of ease. As it was, they died like flies.[44]

The general view was that the horses' share of work
on the battle field was limited to passive suffering. And in
general it seemed as though unless some way could be found
of mitigating the hardship they suffered, cavalry action could
no longer continue to be a part of warfare. Paterson looked
at a trooper of the Scots Greys, exhausted and unshaven, his
uniform dirty, torn and patched, his horse a staggering skeleton
with dull, listless eyes, barely able to move under the weight
of his rider. How could such an animal carry on? 'The next
picture of a cavalry charge you see,' The Banjo wrote, 'put your
foot through it.' He of course knew that his own survival as
a war correspondent depended on having good horses at his
command to carry despatches, and though in French's division
only one horse in three survived, he preserved three in pretty
good health – a saddle-horse, a pack-horse and a cart-horse to
carry heavy goods.

He was by now used to being shot at, and we may
suspect that despite his status as war correspondent, he may
occasionally have fired off a shot or two on his own account,
though he could never admit it publicly. He was also often
standing by the guns as they fired: one of his reports vividly
described an attack by an Australian cavalry column on a group
of enemy horsemen:

With a rush and a clatter and a swing the guns fly past behind the madly straining horses, while the drivers ply their whips, and the men on the limbers with clenched teeth hold to their seats as the guns rock and sway with the pace they are making. 'Action front', and round come the trained horses like machinery, and like lightning the men uncouple the limber and place the gun in position. The range is calculated and the order goes: 'At three thousand. Fuse fourteen. Ready. Fire number one gun!' And with an exulting scream, like a living thing released from prison, away goes the shell across to the little knot of galloping men ... It is a splendid shot, and a buzz of congratulation arises, and a wild feeling of exultation wakes in every man's breast. This is something like sport, this shooting at human game with cannon over three thousand yards of country. 'Hooray! Give 'em another!' The second gun fires and the shell whizzes away, and the same dead silence reigns. When suddenly another note is struck – a discordant note this time. From the rocky tree-covered hill in the direct front only half a mile off comes a clear tock-tock-tock-tock – a couple of clear double reports, and something seems to whistle by the gunners, making a noise, like a heavy wind blowing through a very small crack in the door. Pee-u-u-u-w! It is the thinnest, shrillest sound, this whistle of a bullet at close range. Most of the men duck instinctively as the first bullet goes over. Pee-u-u-u-w! Pee-u-u-u-w! They come by thick enough now, and each man's heart sinks as he sees what the column is let in for. Here we have marched all the guns and horses, without cover, to within half a mile of a hill and the Boers have seized it while we were shooting at their mounted men! Pee-u-u-w! Pee-u-u-w! That fellow was close! ...

Now is the time to see the Royal Horse Artillery at its best! All the years of training, all the hard toil of drilling and practising reap their reward here now. The men serve the guns with machine-like precision; the battery major, with his hands behind his back, stalks up and down behind his guns exactly as a gamecock stalks about his barnyard; there is defiance in every motion as he marches quickly from gun to gun, watching where the shells are landing and giving quick directions as he passes ... 'Shoot, and be damned' is the motto of the R.H.A. 'Let us see who will get sick of it first!' and they send the shells as fast as ever the guns can be worked, whizzing into the hill, where the steady tock-tock-tock-tock still keeps up, and they never flinch, though the hurried white-faced stretcher-bearers run up and carry man after man wounded to the rear.[45]

Paterson never hesitated to involve himself in any action that was taking place anywhere near him, and he was soon widely recognised for the unconventional figure he cut. As one observer, J. H. M. Abbott remembered, writing in the *Sydney Bulletin* after Paterson's death:

He didn't trouble about any sort of uniform, and used to look more like a backveld Dopper than anything else, with several days' growth of dark stubble on his cheerfully saturnine countenance. At a time when the unwritten code of the sentry was 'fire first and challenge afterwards' we often wondered that he didn't

stop a bullet, for he used habitually to turn
up in places most of the scribes were careful
to avoid. One typical story about him relates
to French's cavalry division somewhere
about Modder River on its way to relieve
Kimberley ... A wild-looking man equipped
with a riding switch and only one spur rode
up to the colonel and requested permission to
accompany his corps. 'Who the -------- hell
are *you*?' enquired the CO. 'A. B. Paterson,
sir – representing Reuters and the *Sydney
Morning Herald*.' 'Oh, well – you can come
if you like, Mr Paterson, but I think you're a
damn fool.' With his switch and his sardonic
grin, 'The Banjo' rode in the wake of the
galloping spearmen.[46]

He had at this time some experience of the Boer hero
General Piet Cronje, who had made his reputation during the
first Boer War, besieging the British garrison at Potchefstroom,
and in the second established the sieges of Kimberley and
Mafeking. In February 1900 Cronje was at Magersfontein,
opposing Roberts' army. Failing to prevent the British relief
of Kimberley and retreating eastward, he was surrounded at
Paardeberg, where, after inflicting heavy losses on the British,
he was forced to surrender with about 4,000 men.

The Banjo was getting to know more about the Boers
at first-hand, and added more experience at Paardeberg, where
he witnessed Cronje's surrender. He had been much impressed
by the fact that the Boer general had managed to resist 50,000
men for over a week from a position in open country where he
was continually shelled, lying within a little ring of wagons,
'like a scorpion ringed about with fire'.

After an abortive attack on Cronje's forces by the
Gordon Highlanders and some Canadian troops, the wounded
were being picked up by medical teams when the Boers chose the
very time to surrender. A white handkerchief suddenly appeared

out of a trench, and though at first a trap was suspected, a Boer commander announced that they wanted to surrender.

> They had made up their minds overnight to surrender, as they had no food, but they thought they might just as well repulse the Canadian attack before giving in. They came out of the river bed in dozens and hundreds, all carrying their small belongings – blankets, rugs, bags – as motley a crew as man ever saw. Their clothes ranged from the most tattered moleskin and Crimean wear to really first-class English-cut clothes. Cronje himself, a square-cut farmer-like man, with dark eyebrows and a short beard, was dressed in the outer costume of a long black frock coat, light trousers, tan boots, and a slouch hat. He had his wife and daughter with him in the *laager*,[47] and many others of the Transvaalers had theirs also. They marched out a motley, dirty crew, yet as brave a set of men as ever were born. There were mere boys among them and old men. Each carried his own belongings, and they looked as if they had just come out from a fire, and each was carrying what he had managed to pick up. They were all defiant, and carried their heads high. They knew they had made a phenomenal resistance against the odds – 50,000 men against 3,000.[48]

Among those 3,000, the Banjo encountered one boy of about fifteen, 'a talkative youngster, chattering away volubly. He took himself very seriously, as boys of that age are apt to do. We asked him how long the Boers would go on fighting. He struck an attitude and said: 'Till the last Afrikaner is killed. If there is only he and I left,' he went on, touching the man next him, 'we will fight till we are both killed and then you will have the land. Till then, no.'[49]

He paid tribute too to the Boer women, watching them crawl out from the mud of the trenches, where they had suffered ten days of shelling: 'what such a life must have been is hard to imagine.' In fact, though not one of those correspondents who was inclined to dwell on the horrors of the war – he much preferred the heroics – he was appalled by the conditions the Boers endured at Paardeberg:

> Imagine an area of clear plain about four acres in extent, bordered by a big strong-running river. On this area pack as many bullock wagons, old clothes, arms, ammunition, dead mules, dead bullocks, saddles, boxes, harness, gun carriages, rugs, bedding, and the empty boxes and tins out of a grocery store, intersect it with trenches five feet deep and two feet wide, and fill these trenches with a similar litter, then hurl all these things indiscriminately about till they get well mixed up, and over all, like a cloud, hang a smell, evil beyond credibility, from the decaying animals; populate this Gehenna with three or four thousand people, including dozens of sick and wounded, who scarcely dare leave these trenches day or night, and you have a fair idea of Cronje's *laager* as it has been for the last few days. They were fighting among their sick and wounded, having no place to treat them, except some holes burrowed in the river bank, which they occasionally used as rifle pits. Their women had hidden in some of these burrows from the shells; what such a life must have been is hard to imagine. The rainy season had come on, and their trenches were a sea of mud and slush. Here they had stood ten days' shelling – it was a great performance. The women, black with sun and exposure, were marched out under a row of trees and sat

down, while the men, black, white and yellow, marched in a long row through the camp.[50]

It had been the Prime Minister of Cape Colony, Cecil Rhodes, who had insisted to Roberts on the relief of Kimberly at the earliest moment, forcing him into ordering French into his dangerous gamble, and sacrificing the horses. Paterson was not impressed with Rhodes – to such an extent that he ignored him entirely as far as his dispatches to Australia were concerned. Nor was he keen on Kitchener: 'You could put [his] face on the body of the Sphinx, and nobody would know the difference. He has the aloof air and the fixed expression of a golf champion. His staff say he is all right when you get to know him, but you've got to know him first ...'. Indeed, there seemed times when he had no effect on anyone at all: 'Lord Kitchener came here and stayed a day or two and went on, and hardly a soul knew it till he was away', he remarked on one occasion.[51] He became much more critical after Kitchener had ordered a group of New South Wales riflemen to attack a dangerous *kopje*, though their officer had reminded him that they and their horses had been without food for two days.

Roberts was another matter altogether. Paterson met him for the first time when he came round to inspect some hospital supplies:

> A very small, grizzled old man - they say he is seventy - but he sits his horse like a youngster. Though he is studiously polite to everybody, he has broken several generals already, so the brass hats and the red-collared popinjays of staff officers are wondering, when they go to bed at night, whether their jobs will be gone in the morning ...
>
> Colonel Tom Fiaschi, in charge of our hospital, is a long, gaunt Italian, a celebrated surgeon, and a regular fanatic for hard work. When Roberts came, Fiaschi was operating. Ninety-nine hospital commanders

out of a hundred would have handed over
the job to a subordinate, and would have
gone round with the great man. Not so
Fiaschi. He came to the door of the tent
with his hands all over blood and said:
'You must excuse me, my lord. I am very busy.'
'You are quite right, sir,' said Roberts.
'Go on with your work. I will come round
another time, if you will let me know when it
will suit you.'

Later on, Fiaschi, with a couple of orderlies,
was out looking for wounded in a fog, and
blundered right on to an outlying Boer trench.
'Come on, you men,' said Fiaschi, 'you have
no chance. Give me your rifles.'

The Boers, thinking he had the whole
British Army behind him, handed over their
rifles, and Fiaschi brought them in. This
was reported to Roberts. A staff officer who
handed in the report told me that the old man
said at once:

'Was not that the officer who refused to
come round because he was operating? Give
him a D.S.O.'[52]

One morning at 3 a.m., The Banjo accompanied a
dispatch rider to Roberts' headquarters:

Lord Roberts was sleeping on a little
stretcher in a back room and came out in
his night-shirt to look at them. He doesn't
spare himself, seventy years and all as he is.
He marked each dispatch for the proper staff
officer in the same unhurried, methodical way
in which he gave the Lancers the orders to
stab the niggers. Like Goethe's hero, he works
without haste and without rest. The dispatch
officer introduced me as an Australian

correspondent; and the old man, standing there in his night-shirt, with the weight of the campaign on his shoulders, found time to ask me how the Australians with French were getting on.

'When I first saw the Australians,' he said, 'I thought they were too untrained to be of much use. But the work I have given them to do is the best proof of what I think of them now.'

I told him that the only thing the Australians wanted was more horses. He said: 'That's what everybody wants - more horses.' Then, to the staff officer, 'Make a note of that. Stir up the remount people and let me know what they are doing.'[53]

Paterson had a shrewd eye for character, and thought he knew who could be trusted to run the war, and who was probably more out for self-aggrandisement. He was right more often than not. French and his Chief Staff Officer, Douglas Haig, for instance, he thought made an excellent pair – though he had his reservations:

French and Haig did all the cavalry work and were among the few generals that ever really got in touch with the enemy. Other generals only saw the tails of their horses retreating round a hill. French was like the cat who walked by himself - preferably on the tiles - he had little to say to anybody. In temperament he was like a fox-terrier, always ready to attack the nearest enemy. It was lucky for him that he had the cool, clear-headed Haig at his elbow. Otherwise, he might have walked into a disaster or two that would have left some other general to command the British army in France in the Great War.

As the Tommies put it: 'Haig carried French's brains'. French would take one look at a position and say: I think we'll go up here, Douglas.' But Haig would say: 'I think that's the centre of their position, sir. Suppose we send a patrol up these hills on the right, and get the beggars to shoot a bit. Then we'll know where they are.'

Paterson wasn't particularly impressed by French; he didn't care for Jews, and also disapproved of the General's morals – 'he took all things as they come, especially women'.

The army marched on from the Modder to Poplar Grove, Driefontein and Bloemfontein. Looking towards the city from a hill above it, it appeared completely deserted and peaceful – and in one of the legendary exploits of the war, The Banjo and two friends, one of them the correspondent of the London *Daily News*, simply galloped off towards the town, ahead of the troops. Paterson was never shy of repeating the story, for the rest of his life: 'My Australian-born colt, by Myles-na-Coppaleen, proved himself much better than the other two horses, and we dashed into the town in a string, riding over a lot of rugs and gear of various sorts that the Boers had dropped. Once in the town we slowed to a walk, and were warmly welcomed by the townsfolk, who all shook hands with us, and hoorayed as though they liked having their town captured.'[54] The Mayor suddenly appeared with the Town Clerk and other dignitaries, climbed into a couple of carts, and Paterson and his friends led them out in a surreal procession to surrender the town to Lord Roberts, literally handing him the keys to the public buildings.

Roberts, General French, and his staff, then rode into the town, as cheering townspeople lined the streets – people who, Paterson suggested, would probably have cheered either side in the war. He and his friends then made themselves at home in an extremely comfortable hotel. He was inclined to grow tetchy when anyone else claimed the honour of having been first into Bloemfontein – but was careful also to point out that no danger was involved; the town's council had decided to offer no resistance, and had indeed persuaded the Boers to leave.

Through his private secretary Neville Chamberlain (destined to become the Prime Minister of Britain at the outbreak of the Second World War), Roberts ordered the acquisition of a local newspaper. He re-christened it *The Friend* and approved an editorial committee which included Paterson, Arthur Conan Doyle, and Rudyard Kipling. The Banjo was pleased to meet Kipling, partly no doubt because they enjoyed each others' poems. The Englishman had ostensibly come to South Africa for a holiday after an illness; but Paterson suspected that one did not come to a war zone merely to relax and enjoy a leisurely recovery. More likely, Kipling had come to see what a real war was like, after writing so much about soldiering.

'He is a little, square-built, sturdy man of about forty,' he wrote. 'His face is well enough known to everybody from his numerous portraits; but no portrait gives any hint of the quick, nervous energy of the man. His talk is a gabble, a chatter, a constant jumping from one point to another. In manner, he is more like a businessman than a literary celebrity. There is nothing of the dreamer about him. The last thing anyone could believe is that the little, square-figured man with the thick black eyebrows and the round glasses, is the creator of Mowgli, the Jungle Boy; of *The Drums of the Fore and Aft; of The Man who would be King* ... He talked of little but the war and its results, present and prospective. His residence in America has Americanized his language, and he says "yep" instead of "yes"'.

The Englishman was dogmatic about the future of South Africa: it would prosper. 'There's going to be the greatest demand for skilled labour here the world has ever known. Railways, irrigation, mines, mills, everything would have started here long ago only for this government. The world can't afford to let the Boers have this country to sleep in any longer ...'

But what was to be done with them?

'Give 'em back their farms. But we'll show them how to run the country as it should be run. They don't know what a grand country they have got.'[55]

Paterson was sceptical. Personally, he would hesitate to tell the Boers how to run their country. Kipling was making swift judgements without having the facts. But he was enormously impressed with the character and energy of the man:

> I sat next to him at dinner one night, and he put off the toga of the politician and put on the mantle of the author. It was most fascinating. He yarned away about shoes and ships and sealing-wax and cabbages and kings; interested in everything; asking questions about everything; jumping from one subject to another, from his residence in New York to border battles on the Indian frontier; from the necessity of getting your local colour right, to the difficulty of getting a good illustrator. As he spoke, his face lit up and you began to notice the breadth of his head and the development of the bump of perception over his eyes. His training as a journalist may have made him a bit of an adviser-general to the world at large, but it taught him to talk to anybody and to listen to anybody, for the sake of whatever story they might have to tell. You could have dumped Kipling down in a splitter's camp in the back-blocks of Australia and he would have been quite at home; and would have gone away, leaving the impression that he, was a decent sort of bloke that asked a lot of questions.[56]

The two men parted almost as friends – and were to meet again, later, in quieter circumstances.

Paterson also briefly met Winston Churchill who, then 25, had come out to the Boer War in a fit of pique having been rejected at his first attempt to enter the British Parliament. Within a month, though accredited as a correspondent, and no more (nor less) a combatant than Paterson, he had taken part in the rescue of a train ambushed by the Boers, been taken prisoner, and escaped from a Boer prison with a price on his head. The Banjo first met him afterwards and with typical bravado, Churchill had carried dispatches for his paper through Johannesburg on his bicycle: 'The town was full of Boers drowning the sorrows of their retreat in drink,' noted Paterson; 'If they had recognized him, they would most likely have shot him, as they were a bit out of hand, and he had written some things that they bitterly resented. One must hand it to this Churchill that he has pluck.' The Banjo also noted the young man's aggressiveness - 'He was a man to be feared if not liked' - his swagger, and his overwhelming ambition. He confessed outright that he intended to use the South African campaign for his own purposes: 'This correspondent job is nothing to me,' he said, 'but I mean to get into parliament through it. They wouldn't listen to me when I put up, because they had never heard of me. Now, I am going to plaster the *Morning Post* with cables about our correspondent, Mr Winston Churchill, driving an armoured train, or putting out to Lord Roberts where the enemy is. When I go up for parliament again, I'll fly in.' He pursued this plan to the hilt: after the Duke of Norfolk's horse fell into an ant bear hole, the *Morning* Post arrived with a huge headline: OUR MR WINSTON CHURCHILL SAVES THE DUKE OF NORFOLK FROM BEING CRUSHED BY HIS HORSE. The Banjo commented rather sourly, that as the Duke of Norfolk was the premier Catholic peer of England, Churchill probably thought the story worth thousands of Catholic votes – and was probably right.

The young Englishman was, The Banjo thought, 'the most curious combination of ability and swagger. The army could neither understand nor like him, for when it came to getting anywhere or securing any job, he made his own rules. He had plenty of courage, but like the Duke of Plazo Toro, he felt that he should always travel with a full band. As one general put it: "You never know when you have got Churchill. You can leave him behind in charge of details and he'll turn up at the front, riding a camel, and with some infernal explanation that you can't very well fault."'

The last The Banjo saw of Churchill, he was drinking beer with his cousin the Duke of Marlborough – at breakfast.[57]

He was much impressed, too, by Lieut.-General Hector Macdonald, the so-called 'hero of Omdurman' (Churchill's phrase), and commander of the Highland Brigade during the Paardeberg and Bloemfontein campaigns. Paterson had expected a hard-faced, dour Scotsman, but instead found an enormously attractive, youthful man who looked quite capable of having a good night out and fighting a policeman on the way home without thinking twice about it. 'He yarned away about the Australians at a great rate, and obviously thinks that our troops are quite as good as any for the work here.' The Banjo was astonished and depressed when later Macdonald shot himself, after having been accused of sodomy.

General Roberts decided to remain in Bloemfontein for some time, to rest the troops. Paterson took rooms there and among his dispatches to Sydney, included one of the few, mostly humorous verses he sent home from the war: 'With French to Kimberley':

> He crossed the Reit and fought his way towards
>   the Modder bank.
> The foemen closed behind his march, and hung
>   upon the flank.
> The long, dry grass was all ablaze (and fierce
>   the veldt fire runs);
> He fought them through a wall of flame that
>   blazed around the guns!
> Then limbered up and drove at speed, though
>   horses fell and died;
> We might not halt for man nor beast on that
>   wild, daring ride.
> Black with the smoke and parched with thirst,
>   we pressed the livelong day
> Our headlong march to Kimberley to drive the
>   Boers away.
> He reached the drift at fall of night, and
>   camped across the ford.

Next day from all the hills around the
  Dutchman's cannon roared.
A narrow pass ran through the hills, with guns
  on either side;
The boldest man might well turn pale before
  that pass he tried,
For, if the first attack should fail, then every
  hope was gone:
Bur French looked once, and only once, and
  then he said, 'Push on!'
The gunners plied their guns amain; the hail of
  shrapnel flew;
With rifle fire and lancer charge their squadrons
  back we threw;
And through the pass between the hills we swept
  in furious fray,
And French was through to Kimberley to
  drivethe Boers away.[58]

It was on the march to Kimberley, incidentally, that
Paterson gained his experience not only of managing horses but
of mules – experience which was to serve him well during the
First World War.

He spent only two more months in South Africa. One
gets the impression that having seen the war first-hand, he was
getting bored with what was clearly a forgone conclusion – a
British victory. He and the other correspondents were ordered
by Kitchener to take up advantageous positions from which
to watch his triumphant entry into Johannesburg. Disliking
Kitchener as he did, he more or less ignored the ceremonial
marching of the ten thousand troops, and instead filed a
column about the courage and sturdy determination of his own
'old black Australian horse.' Later he was to write a tribute, in
verse, to the Australian horses which had served so gallantly in
the war. It was published in his collection *Rio Grande's Last Race
and Other Verses*, in 1902, and spoke for the horses on their
'Last Parade':

With never a sound of trumpet,
With never a flag displayed,
The last of the old campaigners
Lined up for the last parade.

Weary they were and battered,
Shoeless, and knocked about;
From under their ragged forelocks
Their hungry eyes looked out.

And they watched as the old commander
Read out to the cheering men
The Nation's thanks, and the orders
To carry them home again ...

'Starving and tired and thirsty
We limped on the blazing plain;
And after a long night's picket
You saddled us up again.

'We froze on the windswept kopjes
When the frost lay snowy-white,
Never a halt in the daytime,
Never a rest at night!

'We knew when the rifles rattled
From the hillside bare and brown,
And over our weary shoulders
We felt warm blood run down ...

'Over the sea you brought us,
Over the leagues of foam:
Now we have served you fairly
Will you not take us home?

'Home to the Hunter River,
To the flats where the lucerne grows;
Home where the Murrumbidgee
Runs white with the melted snows.

'This is a small thing, surely!
Will not you give command
That the last of the old campaigners
Go back to their native land?'

* * * * * *

They looked at the grim commander,
But never a sign he made.
'Dismiss!' and the old campaigners
Moved off from their last parade.[59]

Paterson's own black charger was among the horses left behind, either to be sold off or shot when the war ended. He has sometimes been criticised for not at least rescuing his own horse from that fate; but to have shipped it home privately would have cost a great deal more than he could have possibly afforded. Later in his life on a similar occasion, he was to be even more deeply depressed by the fate of army horses which having done their duty, were deserted and left to be killed or sold off.

Before finally leaving South Africa, The Banjo was to have one more bit of excitement and probably come nearer to death than at any other time during his Boer War adventure. He accompanied General French and the army to Pretoria, which unlike Bloemfontein was not going to fall without a struggle. Paterson found himself at one point caught in what seemed likely to be a fatal trap laid by the Boers: catching a squadron led by Generals French and Porter (the commander of the 1st Cavalry Brigade) on a narrow road from which it was difficult to escape:

> We were like rats in a trap, and if the Boers had advanced they could have shot the whole lot of us, but luckily they contented themselves with driving the advance squadron back. I left the road and took to the rocks, and was retiring as fast as possible, the pony slipping and stumbling over the boulders, when suddenly a bullet struck a rock alongside and

> ricocheted off, and came whizzing, and hit me
> in the ribs, almost hard enough to knock me
> off the horse. I let his head loose then, and he
> went over boulders and stones as if they were
> so much sand, skipping from rock to rock
> like a goat. They say that a frightened rider
> makes a frightened horse, and certainly this
> pony appeared to know that he was expected
> to travel fast ...[60]

The ricochet clearly did no serious damage, and having seen Pretoria successfully occupied, Paterson set out to accompany a force pursuing Christiaan de Wet. He was the commander of a group of commandos which was causing havoc: mining railway tracks and blowing up ammunition trains. De Wet was the most redoubtable of all Boer guerrilla leaders, again and again escaping by the skin of his teeth from British traps, to renew his attacks on isolated British posts. The British in fact never succeeded in capturing him, as Paterson wrote, 'this column is condemned to follow Christiaan de Wet for ever and ever over this interminable veldt'. Catching him was as difficult as putting your finger on a flea, and he seemed likely to die of old age before he was in custody. (He survived to play a reluctant, but active part in the peace negotiations of 1902).

In general, however, the Boers were surrendering in great numbers. Paterson witnessed four thousand of them throwing down their arms, while the British soldiers clustered around them exchanging English pennies for Kruger pennies. His dispatch of 7 September gives another example of his attitude to the native South Africans: 'A nigger began to bawl out some abuse of the Boers, and he was at once tied up and treated to eighteen lashes with the *sjambok* on his bare back. Exeter Hall[61] would, no doubt, be horrified at the idea of the army flogging our poor coloured brethren, but it is the only way to handle niggers.' It is an index of the times that the *Sydney Morning Herald* published the dispatch without demur.

As far as Paterson was concerned, the war was almost over, and there was little point in remaining in South Africa.

He was as a matter of fact mistaken, as there was much more fighting to come. But he had had enough. He took a few days to ride into Basutoland, where he found the peace of the countryside soothing, but suspected that large numbers of Basutos were ready to ride out and poach Boer cattle: they were fine fellows, he thought, and he much admired their capacity for drinking. But he did not stay with them long. He was now eager to get home.

FIVE

To China and England

One of the most interesting things about Paterson's service as a war correspondent is the admiration he subsequently expressed for the Boers and their soldiering. Stung by the British public's denigratory attitude to them when in London in 1902, he published in *Reynold's Weekly Newspaper* a remarkable, bitterly ironical defence of de Wet, Kruger and the rest:

> And the man who upholds any different views,
>   the same is a rotten pro-Boer ...
> And first let us shriek the unstinted abuse that
>   the Tory press prefer —
> De Wet is a madman, and Steyn is a liar, and
>   Kruger a pitiful cur!
> (Though I think if Dom Paul - as old as he is —
>   were to walk down the Strand with his gun
> A lot of these heroes would hide in the sewers or
>   take to their heels and run!
> For Paul he has fought like a man in his days,
>   but now that he's feeble and weak,
> And tired, and lonely, and old and grey, of
>   course its quite safe to shriek!)
> And next let us join in the bloodthirsty shriek,
>   Hooray for Lord Kitchener's bag!
> For the fireman's torch and the hangman's cord
>   — they are hung on the English flag!
> In the front of our brave old Army! Whoop!
>   Their farmhouse blazes bright
> For none of them dress in a uniform, the same
>   as by rights they ought,
> They're fighting in rags and in naked feet, like
>   Wallace's Scotchmen fought!
> (And they clothe themselves from our captured
>   troops — and they're catching them every week;

And they don't hang them — and the shame is
ours, but we cover the shame with a shriek.)

This was in part the attitude he took when lecturing on his experiences during his first months back in Australia. Lecturing was not something he enjoyed doing, or did particularly well; but since he was no longer a solicitor in anything but name, and was not a salaried member of the staff of a newspaper, he had to earn money somehow — and the money he earned from his lectures was good money.

His first lecture was at the Centennial Hall in Sydney on 21 September 1900, accompanied by a 'magic lantern' show. Three days later, at the Town Hall, Sydneysiders saw their first Australian feature film, produced by the Salvation Army. With or without moving pictures, the audiences for The Banjo's Sydney lectures did not always get precisely what they expected. He dealt particularly with the commanding officers, and spent some time passing on their opinion of the Australian troops who had served under them, while what people really wanted was stories of derring-do and Aussie heroism in the field. There were also some attempts to brand him as pro-Boer as he no longer regarded the Boers as 'only partly human'. But after he had conquered his initial nervousness, and got over the self-consciousness of exchanging his war correspondent's gear for evening clothes, he gave good value, and the Sydney lecture was repeated on five following evenings.

Paterson's admiration for General French was obvious. He pointed out that French had gone out of his way to include as many Australians as possible among the picked men he had set aside for special service — including the New South Wales Lancers. His dislike of Kitchener on the other hand was equally transparent and he referred to him not as 'Kitchener of Khartoum' but 'Kitchener of Chaos'. He described him on a visit to wounded soldiers, walking through the wards without a word for anyone and then criticising the sentry for not turning out the guard for him. He was considerably more generous to Haig and Roberts — Roberts in particular.

From Sydney he took his lecture to Parramatta, Newcastle, Melbourne and then to New Zealand, after which he felt ill and exhausted. Nevertheless he was conscious that he was making a great deal of money, and pulling himself together, spoke in north Queensland before returning, worn out, to Sydney and a short rest.

It was this year that his only published novel, *In No Man's Land* (later revised and republished as *An Outback Marriage*) came out at first as a serial in the *Leader*. There is some doubt as to precisely when it was written. A manuscript of some sort existed in 1898, when George Robertson read and criticised it. Clearly he thought it unready for publication, and Paterson presumably worked at it until he at least, felt it was ready for the *Leader*. It wasn't particularly well received or criticised – but Paterson obviously felt that it was worth even more work, and it was to be six years before it was published in book form.

He now accepted an invitation from Sir James Fairfax, an admirer, (who also happened to be the owner of the *Sydney Morning Herald*,) to investigate the plan for a Murrumbidgee River reservoir at Barren Jack. He became an enthusiastic advocate of the scheme and the newspaper supported it until the building of the Burrinjack Dam four years later. But it was another of Sir James' ideas which persuaded The Banjo to give up the vague idea he had of entering politics, and go off once more on his travels.

There is no record of any conversation they may have had about the plan. It is quite possible that Paterson himself put the idea into Sir James's head - but on 27 July 1901 a notice appeared in the *Herald* announcing that 'Mr Paterson intends now to visit China and Japan, and then take the Trans-Siberian Railway to St Petersburg. He will contribute articles to the *Sydney Morning Herald* and the *Sydney Mail*. Those intended for the latter will be accompanied with illustrations, for producing which he will take a photographic outfit. In the event of war breaking out in the East, Mr Paterson will be at hand to act for the *Herald* as occasion may require.'

The Banjo's diary suggests that he was simply inquisitive: 'Everyone thinks that the Russian is an oil-eating vodka-drinking savage, who passes his time trying to shoot the Czar and concocting designs on India. I doubt this altogether and I intend to go and have a look.'[62] But it was no doubt the Boxer Rebellion which attracted his attention to China, where there had been a furious anti-foreign uprising in Shandong. This was organised by the so-called *Yihequan* or 'Righteous and Harmonious Fists', a cult whose members believed that a mysterious boxing art made them invulnerable. At first the Boxers (as they were called in the West), concentrated on killing Chinese Christians and foreign missionaries, but soon moved on to an attempt to destroy everything foreign - including churches, railways, and mines.

By May 1900 the Qing government was secretly supporting the Boxers, then openly called on all Chinese to attack foreigners. Within days, on June 20, the Boxers began an eight-week siege of the foreign legations in Beijing. An international army of some 2,000 men left Tianjin for Beijing but was forced back to Tianjin. This was obviously a first-rate little war, and since discomfort and danger had done nothing to diminish The Banjo's appetite for adventure – indeed, had sharpened it – he immediately saw himself once more as the probing and daring war correspondent.

He may have had another motive: his desire to punch home his view of the Yellow Peril in the Australian Northern Territory. He wrote in the *Herald*:

> If our dashing Australian soldiers are ever to be called upon to fight at all it will be to fight these Eastern peoples, and they will have to fight in our Northern Territory. Judging from South African experience, no civilised power could dream of successful invasion or occupation of any part of our southern coasts; the cost in men, money and transport would be too great. But Japan has over forty millions of people, and they are crowded more closely

together in their islands than the population of Ireland or Scotland. The Russians have one hundred and twenty eight millions, and the completion of the Siberian railway and the 'acquiring' of the Kwangtung province bring them within a few days' steam of us. The Chinese have four hundred millions, all ready to go anywhere and do anything that they are told. Suppose some new Attila arose to lead these hosts ... to take control and organise these vast multitudes? ...

If the Orientals want to come this way they can spare a few millions of people easily enough, and if they sent over enough of an army to hold the north against us for a while they could pour in further people, till before long there would be more yellow people in the north than white in the south.[63]

He had underlined the menace in another article: coastal towns north of Rockhampton were 'hotbeds of Oriental fecundity', there was an eastern quarter in every Queensland coastal town, with Chinese, Japanese, Malays, Cingalese – only a 'wretched remnant' of aboriginals. People said they could do no harm. But they had said that of rabbits.

By the time that article appeared, Paterson was sailing on the Chinese Navigation Company's steamer Changsha for the Celebes, one of the four Greater Sunda islands of Indonesia. From there he went on to Manila, where he attended a race meeting and interviewed General Adna Romanza Chaffee, who had commanded the American forces at the liberation of Peking during the Boxer rebellion. Then it was on to Hong Kong, the harbour of which he described in a vivid colour piece for the Herald:

There were fleets of junks, hundreds of them in each fleet. We must have passed three or four thousand junks in one day, and each junk has five or six men aboard. The refrigerating engineer says, 'It's a fair masterpiece how they all live.' They carry no barometers, but they all know when a typhoon is coming as well as most scientific navigators, and they hustle for shore like chickens running to shelter from a hawk. Sometimes the big deep sea steamers run over them in the night, and then there is a crash and a yell out of the darkness, and the big boat goes on, as no one particularly wants a visit from all the mates of the runover junk.[64]

En route to Shanghai, the *Changsha* passed thousands of junks, and in the Yangtze itself there was a congestion of junks, merchant ships and warships such as Paterson had never seen. How could things go on peacefully with so many nations jockeying for advantage, he wondered? He was convinced that it would be impossible for people of five or six different nationalities to live peacefully together. He would have found the idea of modern, multi-ethnic Australia not only a strange, but a totally unbelievable proposition. He might write 'We are all Australians now',[65] but multi-nationalism was *not* what he meant.

He took a brief walk or two about the Shanghai streets and in the evening a rickshaw man took him round the gambling dens, opium shops and theatres – 'music halls quite on the England plan', but 'terrible opium dens, the wan figures of Chinamen seen through an evil-smelling mist.' The following morning, inevitably, he made straight for the race-course, where he was fascinated by the small Chinese ponies from the north – 'as vicious a little brute as stands on four feet: he will deliberately attack his owner if he gets him at a disadvantage, and even his *marfoo* has to exercise the greatest caution in going near him. A stranger can only get on him by "stalking" him behind the *marfoo* and sneaking on to his back while the pony is intently watching the *marfoo* in hopes of being able to plant a blow with his front feet in the *marfoo's* ribs.'[66]

His next stop via a Russian coaster, was Cheefoo (now called Yantai). By the Chefoo Convention, signed in 1876, many new treaty ports had been established, and partly as a consequence the town became a ferment of espionage with spies from all over the east – but especially Russia and Japan - jostling for position. Ambitious to go on to St Petersburg, he sought out the Russian consul who told him that the railway line was blocked, and that at least for the time being he had better remain in Cheefoo. Happily there was a race-track, and the consul kindly invited Paterson to ride one of his ponies, Gilyak, in a race. Gilyak was a bit of a problem, 'a stupid, uncivilised brute' which Paterson managed to mount only after the horse's head had been inserted into a bag.

He easily took the lead in the race, but as soon as he saw no-one ahead of him, the horse slowed down to give the others a chance and Paterson could do nothing with him. It later turned out that the horse wasn't Gilyak at all, but a Manchurian pony that a dealer had bought for three pounds ten and passed off as the animal for which the Russian consul had paid $120.

In Cheefoo Paterson the journalist took the opportunity of visiting the well-known authority on China, George E. Morrison - 'Chinese Morrison'. He was an Australian-born journalist who had trained as a doctor but spent years travelling in America, the West Indies and finally the Far East, where he had become a special correspondent for the London *Times* and was recognised as an expert in eastern affairs.

There was clearly a clash of personality as Morrison rambled on too much, often Paterson thought, irrationally, and moreover he spent too much time talking rather loosely about women, something Paterson never did, and hated others for doing. However, he did rather agree with Morrison's theory that Australia should have ignored the Boer War, and instead have walked into China and 'taken the boss mandarin's seat at the top of the table.' And he certainly approved of Morrison's way of dealing with the Chinese, which was never to allow a Chinaman to assume for a moment that he was in any way the white man's equal.

Assured that the line to St Petersburg was impassable, and would remain so through the Siberian winter, The Banjo gave up the whole idea of his ambitious journey and instead set sail back to Hong Kong, where he picked up a P&O liner bound for Southampton. It was an entertaining voyage, for the great English music-hall star Marie Lloyd joined the ship at Singapore, on her way home from a tour of Australia with her husband Alec Hurley, a singer of 'Ccoster' songs. Her witty, sexy act had first bemused then delighted audiences, contradicting as it did any idea of the English stage as the home only of classic theatre. One would not have expected the plump, blousy, sexy Marie and the wiry, ascetic Paterson to get on – but they clearly liked each other, and in *Happy Dispatches* Paterson wrote an affectionate sketch of her:

> She walks into a room as a dreadnought steams into a harbour, followed by a fleet of smaller vessels in the shape of sycophants and hangers-on. Her conversation consists mostly of epigram and innuendo. For instance, a lady passenger, travelling by herself, has her belongings shifted across the ship to a new cabin every time that the wind changes, and there is talk of favouritism: 'Ho, what are yer goin' to do about it,' says Marie. 'She sits at the purser's table, don't she?'
>
> A wealthy Greek passenger - quite an old man - is always hanging round a very pretty young girl, who is one of Marie's entourage. Then his attentions cease abruptly. After dinner one night Marie gives me the key to the situation: 'That old Greek,' she says. 'Do you know what he had the cheek to do? Did you ever hear anything like it? He wanted to take the little girl on a trip with him through Egypt, the old vagabond!'

'And what did you say to him?' I ask, confident that Marie must have said something worthy of the occasion.

'What did I say to him? "Let's see your cheque-book," I says. 'That's what I said to him.'

Some officers' wives from India asked a solitary male passenger if he would mind moving a few places up the table, so that they could sit together; and Marie had a few words to say on that subject.

'They asked yer to change yer seat, did they? Well, a thing like that would kill me dead, that would - stone dead. D'yer know what I'd ha' said to 'em? I'd ha' said, "Excuse me, but perhaps when you come out before you must have came in the steerage. You ain't used to travellin' first-class saloon." That's what I'd ha' said.'

Learning that I am some sort of literary person, Marie asks me to write her a song, and adds that she has paid as much as a pound and thirty bob for some of her song hits in London. Then she lets her eye rove over the deck where the passengers are walking in pairs, male and female, as the Lord created them.

'There you are,' she says, 'all you want is a good ketchline! What about "They've all got their little bit o' muslin." Ow would that go?'

One can't help thinking it would have gone very well indeed, but sadly the song never materialised. Later, when the ship stopped at Marseilles, The Banjo heard that there were races, and he and Marie made up a party. She learned that, world-famous though indeed she was, she was not quite sufficiently well-known in Marseilles.

All the public stands were packed, and it was impossible to see anything. But there was any amount of room on an official stand marked *defendu*, and Marie picked on a young Canadian member of our party to escort her up into this stand. We told her that *defendu* meant no admittance, but she said she was going up, anyway. 'If he tells 'em I'm Marie Lloyd it'll be all right,' she said.

At the top of the stairs her escort was grappled by a gendarme about the size of a weevil, and the pair of them rolled down the stairs with the gendarme's little red legs flashing in the air every time he came uppermost. Nor was it a silent film, for the gendarme yelled, *à moi mes camarades* every time that he hit a fresh step. It took the combined efforts of three gendarmes to secure the Canadian.

The gendarmes were going to put the Canadian in the coop, but he explained that neither he nor his lady friend knew any French, so they embraced him and let the pair of them stop on the stand.

Sitting up there in comfort among the French aristocracy, Marie scorned to notice the rest of her fellow passengers milling about among the plebeian crowd below. When they came down the stairs, she said to her escort: 'It's a pity you couldn't speak French, you could ha' told 'em who I was.'

'I can speak French all right,' he said. 'I'm a French Canadian, and I can speak better French than any of these coves. But you didn't want to get locked up, did you?'

Marie was so impressed that she fumbled in her bag and gave him a card, marked 'Admit one,' to the stalls on the opening night of her season in London.[67]

The Banjo arrived in London on a typical winter's day – 'the whole city choking in a kind of yellow gloom, out of which the whistles of the bus conductors and the shouts of cabmen rose like the din of fiends in a pit of torment. The theatres nearly all closed their doors. Trafalgar Square was full of buses all night; buses that had failed to make their way home, and simply pulled up and waited for daylight, with their passengers huddled inside; the cabmen wouldn't even try to take people home – a five-pound note was vainly offered by one man for a drive of half an hour – what would have been half an hour's drive if there had been any light, or even any decent sort of darkness to drive by; but this awful yellow shroud choked everything; and yet, talking it over with an English bus driver next morning he said with the greatest pride, "Ah! You don't see fogs like that in no other part of the world!" '[68]

Paterson found the English political world a puzzle, especially the determined way in which the decisions of Government were kept secret. 'England and Australia are at the two extremes in political matters,' he wrote in the *Herald* of 11 January. 'Here a general may half wreck an Empire and no one does anything; with us if a sergeant of Volunteers is disrated for drunkenness there is a Labour member to demand a special committee of the House to inquire into it. Those are the two systems, and each has its drawbacks. You may spend your money and don't have any choice.'

He was surprised and depressed at the fact that nobody in England had any interest at all in Australia or what went on there. He made an attempt to persuade The Times to appoint him as their Australian correspondent, in the hope of at least beginning to put things right. At the end of November he wrote George Robertson to announce that he had been interviewed and the appointment was all but made, though the Editor's one idea was that the visit of the Duke of York to Australia 'marked an epoch in the history of the country ... I longed to say, "Yes, he got nearly as big a reception as Bill Beach, the skuller." '

But nothing came of the notion. The Banjo was pleased that some Australian artists had had success in Europe, and renewed his acquaintance with Phil May, the English cartoonist and caricaturist who had spent some time in Sydney. May took him to a number of clubs and parties, and he even contributed a set of verses to the Pink Un, the famous London racing paper – in which he enthused about the speed of the motor car, and its capacity for carnage:

> *We outpace, we outlast, we outstrip!*
> *Not the fast-fleeing hare,*
> *Nor the racehorses under the whip,*
> *Nor the birds of the air*
> *Can compete with our swiftness sublime,*
> *Our ease and our grace.*
> *We annihilate chickens and time*
> *And policemen and space.*
>
> *Do you mind that fat grocer who crossed?*
> *How he dropped down to pray*
> *In the road when he saw he was lost;*
> *How he melted away*
> *Underneath, and there rang through the fog*
> *His earsplitting squeal*
> *As he went - Is that he or a dog,*
> *That stuff on the wheel?* [69]

One of the more interesting events of his relatively short stay in the mother country was a weekend with Kipling at The Elms, the author's house on the village green of the pleasant little village of Rottingdean, near Brighton on the Sussex coast. There Kipling had recently read the proofs of the first part of *Kim*, and was at work on the *Just So* stories. Once more, as in South Africa, they got on very well, and Kipling said he was seriously thinking of buying a house in Australia – to add to the ones he already owned in Cape Town and New York.

His view of Australia remained, however, that its people had not grown up yet, and thought the Melbourne Cup the most important thing in the world. The Banjo was unable to shake this conviction, but was amused when stopping at a butcher's to buy a side of lamb, Kipling instructed the tradesman that he must 'buy all the Australian lamb he could, and keep the money in the Empire.' The butcher was unimpressed: 'The Empire! Ho! My customers don't worry about the Empire – its their guts they think about.'

But The Banjo and Kipling continued to find that they had much in common. Kipling too was an observer, even of matters of which he had little understanding. Paterson much admired a couple of lines from one of his poems (relating needless to say, to horses):

> The dun he leaned against the bit and slugged
>   his head above,
> But the red mare played with the snaffle-bars,
>   as a maiden plays with a glove.

He asked Kipling how he, a non-horseman, had come up with such a vivid and fitting image. 'Observation', Kipling replied.

Paterson left England in early spring without a great deal of regret, if we are to trust the lines he wrote as his boat edged out into the English Channel:

> The London lights are far abeam
> Behind a bank of cloud,
> Along the shore the gas lights gleam,
> The gale is piping loud;
> And down the Channel, groping blind,
> We drive her through the haze,
> Towards the land we left behind –
> The good old land of 'never mind',
> And old Australian ways.
>
> The narrow ways of English folk
> Are not for such as we;
> They bear the long-accustomed yoke
> Of staid conservancy:
> But all our roads are new and strange
>
> And through our blood there runs
> The vagabonding love of change

> *That drove us westward of the range*
> *And westward of the suns.*[70]

He was back in Sydney in April, and had barely begun to write again for the *Sydney Morning Herald* when he was off on a fascinating journey to the New Hebrides - the colonial name for the group of islands now known as Vanuatu. The head of the Australian firm of Burns, Philip & Co., Sir James Burns, asked him to accompany a group of volunteers aiming to settle on the islands. The firm had bought thousands of acres from the natives, paying for them with goods of one sort and another. But the French had also bought land there, frequently from the same chiefs, who had no scruples about taking money from invaders of any nationality. As a result squabbles of every kind had broken out – about ownership, boundaries, the rights of particular chiefs to sell particular slices of land ... Discussions between the French and Australians were relatively civilized, but the natives tended to believe that the sharper their knives were, the sooner disputes would be over.

Sir James had come to the conclusion that first come should be first served, and persuaded a group of volunteers to brave the verbal attacks of the French and the more insistent attacks of the natives. If they survived both, they would receive their land free. Would Paterson go along with them and observe events?

It sounded an adventure too interesting to be resisted: the Federal Government approved of it, and the *Sydney Morning Herald* would accept any articles he might send back, providing a useful addition to the fee Sir James was willing to pay. Paterson found the Australian Pilgrim Fathers, as he called them, a fascinating lot: shearers, miners, prospectors, farmers - men from the outback. Some of them had decided to join the expedition for reasons which are well understood today: one man said that on his New South Wales farm he had seen only three inches of rain in nine months. If the seasons were good, he couldn't make much, while if they were bad he lost everything. Another had been made redundant by the Queensland Government. 'It seems hard,' Paterson thought, 'that with all the land we have in Australia these very desirable colonists should have to leave our country to hunt in other lands for that living which they ought surely to be able to find in their own.'

The little party of adventurers left Sydney on 31 May, with eighteen settlers provided with $200 each, and a small group of missionaries provided with Bibles. They were all much impressed by the fecundity of Howe Island and then of Norfolk Island, and some of them showed signs of wanting to settle down in one or the other.

On Norfolk, Paterson recalled Marcus Clarke's famous novel For the Term of his Natural Life, and wandered among the melancholy roofless ruins of the old barracks and prisons, wondering 'how many poor wretches had tramped in over the same grey flagstones, how many had looked wearily up at the now ruined wall where the clock used to be, how many times the gangs, ironed together, had passed clanking out of those doors to their daily work up on the green hills yonder.'[71]

But he was fascinated too by the present-day islanders, tough men and rather frail women, and by the little native horses which grazed on the almost perpendicular cliffs, and were so strong and agile he believed they could climb up the side of a well pulling a cart after them.

The voyage itself provided Paterson with some excellent comic material, especially when a 'lady passenger' came on board. When she went to the bathroom and turned on the water, she got 'a stream of cockroaches, all in the highest health and spirits. They fled in various directions, drying their whiskers as they went.' Of the lady passenger he gave no further news.

By mid-June they had landed at Vila, the chief town of the New Hebrides, and were delighted that there seemed to be no end to the richness of the soil and what would grow in it – from bananas to coffee, spices to maize. Perhaps surprisingly the Australian and French settlers got on very amicably, but the newcomers suffered from a great deal of trepidation about the natives, who they believed to be cannibals. On their first trek into the jungle a naked savage suddenly appeared carrying a rifle, and the settlers did their best to hide behind what trees were available. The man fumbled in the strip of leather which passed for a belt, and politely asked if anyone had change for four shillings. Paterson soon discovered that though many of the natives had rifles, they were unable to hit a barn unless they were actually inside it.

He was able to report to Sir James Burns that all was likely to go well. Which for a time it did, until tariff barriers put an end to the export market. But that was long after The Banjo had left the islands.

It was at about this time that Paterson was associated for a while with Miles Franklin, the author of *My Brilliant Career*. This archetypal Australian book written by a 15-year-old girl brought up in the Bush, is now a classic; but when it came out in 1901, it sold only just over a thousand copies in Australia and under four hundred in England. Now she was trying to sell her second book, tentatively entitled *The Outside Track*. Presumably knowing that Paterson was not only a fellow author but also a solicitor, she wrote asking for his advice about publishing agreements. She also sent him her second manuscript, about which he was unenthusiastic.

But he did attempt to help her sell some short stories, and she suggested they might collaborate on a play. He agreed, and they exchanged letters about the idea, Paterson insisting that the piece should not attempt to be 'clever', but should be full of sweat and tears and swearing, and have a really hateful villain 'so black that charcoal wouldn't leave a mark on him.' It would do no harm, too, to have a daughter whose family had thrown her out for bringing shame on their name.

The synopsis he finally sent her does not offer much evidence that the world has lost a masterpiece. It was set in Camelot and the plot involved King Arthur, Queen Guinevere, Sir Lancelot and the usual suspects, with Mordred trying to poison the King and imprisoning the Queen in a deep, dank dungeon. At this stage, Miles withdrew – partly it seems because people were beginning to link her name romantically with Paterson's. They had certainly on paper been for a while the closest of friends, and The Banjo – who was not making a great deal of money at this time – sent her the occasional five pound note. She sent the last one back, clearly fearing that they were growing too close and four years later she left Australia to become an important figure in the American Women's Trade Union movement.

Meanwhile Paterson was working hard without great financial success. He travelled about quite a lot for both the *Sydney Morning Herald* and *The Bulletin*, and was writing occasionally for *The Pastoralists' Review*. Then he was trying to get together his occasional pieces about the Boer War in the hope of publishing a book about the part played in it by Australians. The one really positive event of the period was his meeting, in Tenterfield, with Alice Walker, the young daughter of a local farmer. They fell in love – and this time, the engagement was not to last seven years.

SIX

The Banjo and The Breaker

Rio Grande's Last Race, The Banjo's second collection of poems, was published on 24 November 1902. Both he and his publisher were slightly concerned about its quality. Robertson even commissioned an outside reader to advise whether there were any verses below the standard of those in *The Man from Snowy River*. They need not have been worried - the first edition promptly sold out, and Australian reviewers particularly praised the 'genial fun' of the verses and the gusto of the ballads.

As the book was hurried into print, Paterson was at work on material which he was to contribute to a book entitled *The Story of South Africa*. He wrote about the part played by the Australian and New Zealand troops, and the problems experienced with the horses. In these he dealt not only with the dreadful suffering of the beasts, the reasons for it and how it could have been avoided, but also with the tactical uses of the horses in warfare and how the whole theory of the use of cavalry must be adjusted in the age of the long-range, quick-firing rifle.

In many ways the most extraordinary event of the year to affect him, if not directly, took place in South Africa. News arrived in Sydney in early March that two Australian officers had been found guilty of murder and executed and one of them was his old acquaintance, Harry 'Breaker' Morant. In the days when news-gathering and dissemination moved at a relative snail's-pace, almost every account of the events leading up to The Breaker's court martial and execution differed from the next. On 4 April the *Sydney Morning Herald* published a story from its unnamed correspondent to the effect that Lieutenants Morant and P. J. Handcock, of the Bushveldt Carbineers, an irregular British force, had been tried by court martial at Pietersburg in January, been found guilty of the murder of several Boer prisoners of war, and of a clergyman, the Rev. Predicant Heese, and been sentenced to death. A third officer had also been found guilty, but the sentence of death had been commuted to penal servitude.

The story was repeated in various garbled forms over the next weeks, and it was some time before a version of the true facts emerged. The press – even *The Bulletin*, which had published so many of his verses - immediately painted Morant as the blackest of villains, an effete Englishman who had pretended to know something about the bush, and 'had not even the conscience to remain in England and live the life of what is known as an upper middle-class English gentleman.'

On 12 May, certainly before he could have had any idea of the facts in the case, Paterson wrote a piece for the *Sydney Mail* recalling The Breaker as a man who 'feared nothing but hard work ... the hardships he went through to avoid working were much more formidable than the work itself would have been.' Popular for his dash and courage, he was a spectacularly good horseman, kind-hearted and good-natured and an enemy to no-one but himself.

'Those who knew him best', argued The Banjo, 'say that he would sooner have given a sick Boer the coat off his back than shoot him for any money – especially Transvaal money – that he might have about him ... Such as he was he was the same to all men. With a good commander over him he might have made a fine soldier. As it turned out he got into exactly the worst company that a man of his temperament could have met.'

Paterson went on to send *The Bulletin* some of the letters The Breaker had written him years ago, and a contribution of his own in which he said he found it very difficult to think of Morant as a murderer. The paper hastily turned about: maybe the whole thing had been a dreadful misunderstanding. However, it was not, and after talking to as many people as possible about the case, Paterson came to the reluctant conclusion that The Breaker's fellow Carbineers had been speaking the truth when they accused Morant and his co-defendants of being 'actuated by lust for loot in Land, Cattle and Gold' and cold-bloodedly planning 'to wipe out the holders of certain farms which they hoped to get for themselves after the war in return for "distinguished service" '. Some of the murdered men had been school-teachers and one a Red Cross worker. The Banjo also heard, first-hand, an account of how Morant, meeting a man driving across country in a cart, had pulled him down and shot him. Unfortunately he turned out to be a Dutch clergyman

Paterson repeated this story and the accusation that Morant had put himself about as a hero, telling tall tales about his heroism while serving with Lord Roberts at Kimberley, Paardeberg and Bloemfontein. None of these stories was true - he had spent most of his time in South Africa acting as a 'runner' carrying dispatches for a London *Daily Telegraph* correspondent (he later claimed himself, to be the paper's correspondent). As to the murders, it was Morant's fellow Australians who had dobbed him in, writing to their commanding officer insisting that the rumours about the murders committed by Morant and his friends should be investigated, for 'many of us Australians who have fought throughout nearly the whole war ... cannot return home with the stigma of these crimes attached to our names.'

The truth of the affair was slow to come out, and the facts are still to some extent in question. The original records of the courts-martial which opened on 16 January 1902 vanished not long after they were concluded. The only full account we have was written some time after the events by one of the accused, George Witton. Morant it seems never denied that he ordered eight prisoners-of-war to be executed, but argued that he did so because his senior officer, Capt. Percy Hunt, had ordered the company to take no prisoners. He himself had been commanded to issue this order 'by Pretoria'. Hunt had been killed by Visser, a Boer commando who mutilated Hunt's body and whose execution was thus a justifiable reprisal. Asked whether he had set up a proper court-martial like the one before which he was appearing, The Breaker replied:

'Was it like this? No - it was not quite so handsome. As to rules and regulations, we had no Red Book, and knew nothing about them. We were out fighting the Boers, not sitting comfortably behind barbed-wire entanglements; we got them and shot them under Rule 303.' 'Rule 303' referred to the .303 calibre Lee-Enfield rifles he and the other Carbineers carried.

Morant was not inclined to take his trial calmly: he threatened to subpoena Lord Kitchener himself and question him about the 'take no prisoners' order. It did him no good. The court was adjourned to consider its verdict – but no verdict was announced, and a second trial opened on 31 January. This time the three men were accused of shooting a further eight Boer prisoners, murdering a Boer member of the Carbineers (Trooper Van Beuren, who they wrongly suspected of being a spy) and murdering a German missionary, the Rev. Predicant Heese. Morant was said to have either shot Heese or ordered him to be shot, (there were no eyewitnesses), and it seems quite likely that Heese was in fact killed by a Boer sniper. The case against The Breaker for this murder was withdrawn.

The defence tried to argue that the killings were not murder because of the 'take no prisoners' order, but were unable to prove that any such order was in fact given. There were suspicions that Lord Kitchener did indeed issue it and that this was covered up because it was clearly against the rules of war. As it was, Morant and Handcock were found guilty and sentenced to death by firing squad. Witton was also condemned, but his sentence commuted, and indeed he was later released from custody.

The trials, if they can be described as trials, were extraordinarily casual affairs. The accused men, Morant, Handcock and Witton, far from being imprisoned were allowed to come and go as they pleased, and Witton even attended a cricket match where he was seen by the president of the court, who was surprised to see a man whose death warrant he had just signed. Perhaps even more astonishingly, while the trials were under way the three accused were released from their cells and given arms in order to help repel an attack on Pietersburg. It is said that they fought bravely, but it made no difference. 'Breaker' Morant and Handcock were executed by firing squad on 27 February 1902. Morant declined to see a clergyman, declaring himself to be a Pagan. He also refused to be blindfolded, and his last words were, famously, 'Shoot straight, you bastards! Don't make a mess of it!'

The Banjo's part in the matter was peripheral – he wrote about the affair without any special knowledge of the facts, and perhaps over-hastily. He was certainly criticised in some quarters for being too quick to condemn his former colleague and friend. Indeed before the courts-martial, he had actually dismissed the charge against The Breaker for the shooting of the Padre and wrote ignorantly of the callous way in which Morant pulled Heese out of his cart and shot him. He also gave the impression of throwing off his acquaintanceship with Morant, and failed to mention The Breaker's talent as a balladeer. Indeed, a correspondent to the *Sydney Morning Herald* rebuked him publicly for this. Perhaps with his own code of being true to one's friends, he might have been less hasty and more charitable. In any event, whatever he felt about Morant and the whole incident, it must have considerably discomfited him.

In January 1903 his life took a new turn when the proprietors of the *Sydney Evening News* offered him the editor's chair. The idea of being more or less permanently stuck in an office in Sydney surely cannot have appealed to him. Though he had spent his life until then racketing about, and indeed had complained to Miles Franklin that he was 'weary to death of sleeping in railway trains and bush public houses,' he was always basically a man of action. But maybe he was now thinking of settling down – for soon he was to have a wife to support and in time two children, a boy and a girl. He accepted the offer.

Founded in 1867 by a Cornish immigrant, the *Evening News* had become by 1903 very much a part of Sydney's political, cultural and social life. It was a serious rival to the *Sydney Morning Herald*, carrying parliamentary reports and business news as well as the usual stories about daily events. When its third editor died suddenly, Paterson must have seemed a fairly obvious choice to succeed him; he had a reputation as a reporter at large, but at the same time had training in the law and was clearly a serious character. Moreover his widely popular ballads of the bush represented him as an Australian who knew what it meant to be an Australian.

Newly appointed newspaper editors today seem to make a lot of changes from the moment they take office. They generally uproot the regular contributors and replace them with what they see as 'new blood'. They like to re-design the newspaper in line with what is apprehended as the latest taste in typography and the latest fashion in design. The Banjo left this well alone, at least for the first few months. Gradually, however, he did make changes, tending to favour any reports concerning the army, encouraging articles and correspondence on the history of Sydney, and engaging one of the first political cartoonists to work in the city.

He did not radically alter the design of the paper, which followed closely the pattern established in London many years prior. It had small advertisements on the front page rather than headlines and no sports news on the back page, just more advertisements. Political news was on page four, with sedate leading articles commenting on the chief topics discussed in Parliament. There was however plenty of room for accounts of sensational murders and suicides, and page five had a rather daring column reporting 'Today's Divorces'. Paterson's main change during his first year – and anyone who knew him might have foretold this – was to turn page two into a comprehensive sports page, with horse-racing heavily emphasised (represented also on the leader page by the daily 'Randwick Track Notes').

It was three months after his appointment as editor that he married. His bride, Alice Emily Walker, was twenty-five and The Banjo fourteen years her senior. As the daughter of a grazier, Alice had virtually grown up in the saddle and was a competent horsewoman. This no doubt endeared her to her husband, as did her quiet and submissive temperament. Paterson's sister Jessie found her 'a very nice girl' and 'a very good housekeeper'.[72]

The wedding took place in the nonconformist church at Tenterfield, and was particularly unostentatious, with a very small reception at the station attended only by the immediate families and a very few close servants. The honeymoon was spent at Cooma, the gateway to the Snowy Mountains, and Bombala, midway between the mountains and the south coast. Then it was back to Sydney and West Hall, where their daughter Grace was born in 1904, and their son Hugh Barton in 1906. It was also back to work at the newspaper office.

The general view is that Paterson was not a great editor and very possibly not even a good one, at least when it came to the business of knowing what did and did not make news. The reporters who worked for him accused him of having no idea of news values. Most of the time, it was suggested, he sat in his office looking bemused and disorientated, his roll-top desk covered with pieces of paper which had to be brushed to the floor if he wanted himself, to write anything. The one trait for which his contributors admired and liked him was his generosity – born no doubt of his memory of what it was like trying to make a living by contributing the occasional set of verses at seven-and-six a time.

But that was a view of reporters for whom news was the whole point of a newspaper. Paterson took the view that there was more to life than hard news, and much of the *Evening News* read very like one of today's newspaper supplements. Often his own contributions, such as his poems and satires on political life, were prominently displayed, and lively feature articles such as his reporting of the 'motor reliability trial' run between Sydney and Melbourne in February 1905. This was one of his liveliest pieces of writing:

> In those days the roads beyond Goulburn were crossed here and there by steep gutters to drain off the water. They were quite invisible from a distance, and all the experienced drivers had their passengers standing up on the back seats to yell out 'gutter' when one hove in sight. A poor little Frenchman named Maillard, who had taken part in some of the big motor races in France, was a hot favourite for the event. He was driving a De Dion, and beat everybody to Goulburn. On leaving

Goulburn he went past the other cars like an express train, but unfortunately he had no knowledge of Australian roads ... and hit the first gutter at fifty miles an hour, sending his car up in the air like a hurdle horse which has hit a jump. Parts of the car were scattered all over the road, and the Frenchman ran from one to another shouting: *'Pourquoi les canivaux?'* (why are the gutters there?). As I had some sort of Surry Hills knowledge of French, I did my best to explain things, but the only result was to make him cry worse than ever.

A Melbourne stock-broker, having his first long drive, had a first-class 'cockatoo' standing up in the back of his car (cockatoos always get a sentinel to look out for trouble) and did so well between Goulburn and Gundagai that he insisted on shouting champagne for all the drivers and their associates. Nothing like this had happened in Gundagai since the big flood, and, as soon as the word got round, the whole population of the town drifted into the bar and started to lap up champagne like milk. He drank with all and sundry and did himself so well that when he left Gundagai next morning the bridge was not wide enough for him and he hit the abutment fair and square with his radiator. This car, also, became a casualty; but the owner said that if a man was a sport it was up to him to *be* a sport and he insisted on having the car repaired at Gundagai so that he could save his face with his friends by finishing the trial, even if everybody else had weighed in and gone home when he arrived. Sad to say, the local blacksmiths were unequal to a repair job which practically meant taking the tail light and building a new car on to it. He and his 'cockatoo' passed us somewhere about Seymour, sitting on the remains of their car in a railway truck, waving bottles, and shouting encouragement.

Other drivers were Charley Kellow, once a track cyclist and, later on, famous as the owner of Heroic; Harrie Skinner, of Tivoli Theatre fame; and a death-or-glory boy whose name I cannot remember, but who was out to beat everybody for speed and hang the consequences. He was driving a Renault and, coming to a partly-opened railway gate, he opened it the rest of the way by hitting it with his car, thus saving perhaps half a minute but bending his axle. He was the last to leave and the first to arrive at every control but he lost the reliability competition because of his bent axle. He said that he never expected to win it, anyhow, as he was not using the brand of tyres favoured by the promoters. We, ourselves, needed no such specious excuse, as we lost our chance by taking a wrong road neat Tarcutta. We did not go 20 yards in the wrong road; but just to avoid going back those 20 yards we took a short cut across some long grass, apparently smooth, but it was like the Goulburn Road.

Somebody had dug a deep drain across it - a drain hidden by the long grass, like one of those pits they dig to catch wild animals in Africa. Bang, went some spokes of a wheel, but there were three perfectly good wheels left. Some flour-mill mechanics at Albury bolted stout timber supports on to either side of the wheel, and with many stoppages we got into Melbourne just before the speeches of welcome were quite finished.

Such was motoring in those days. Every horse that saw us, kept his tail up and bolted across country like a wallaby. If attached to a trap, so much the worse for the trap! At our stoppages en route the rude forefathers of the various hamlets would come up and put their hands on the radiator, to see whether it was hot; which it generally was - sometimes very hot. One of these veterans made all his following put their pipes out, lest the car should blow up. Yet, the last time that a car stuck me up on that road, a twelve-year-old boy got off a passing cart and put it right! The world moves, even if sometimes in the wrong direction.[73]

The Banjo's only real objection to the horseless carriage was that it frightened the horses, and his chief fear that the quality of Australian roads would be improved to the point that cars would commonly travel here as quickly as he had seen them travel in England, between London and Brighton. They were great clouds of dust rolling over the countryside 'like the pillar of fire that guided the Israelites but a trifle faster.'

It was in November that his novel, *In No Man's Land*, was at last published in book form as *An Outback Marriage*. (It had been published six years previously as a newspaper serial).) He had done quite a lot of revision since it originally came out, but not enough to save it from ultimate oblivion. Its convoluted plot remained almost impenetrable - about an Englishman Jim Carew, who comes to Australia in search of a man from whom he hopes to inherit a large property. This is run alongside another story of a failed solicitor, Gavan Black. Black needs to marry money and has designs on an English heiress, Marty Grant, who has come out to run Kuryong, her father's New South Wales station.

The story does not for a moment carry a great deal of conviction, and what value the novel has, relies entirely on Paterson's descriptions of bush life. The *Australasian* called these 'as good as anything in Australian fiction', and to an extent that is true, for The Banjo made excellent use of his knowledge of horsemanship and the ways of the drovers, and indeed of some incidents in his own life, such as buffalo-hunting in the Northern Territory. Although the horses are real enough, however, the humans are poorly characterised. For The Englishman's conversation is spiced with 'Eh, what?' and 'Don't you know?' making him a complete caricature, and though this cannot be said of his Australian characters, they are far from sharply drawn. Colin Roderick in his biography of Paterson identifies which people Paterson based the characters on – members of the Barton family, Paterson's aunt Nora, and others. He also asserts that Kuryong, the New South Wales station which figures in the story, is clearly based on Boree Nyrang. But the novel only just bears reading.

An Outback Marriage sold a thousand copies reasonably easily, but then sales fell away, forcing Paterson to conclude, rightly, that he would never make a living as a novelist. Putting aside a racing story which he had been working on in a desultory fashion for some time, he concentrated on another long-term project. This was a collection of bush songs which Robertson had been encouraging him to complete for almost ten years. *Old Bush Songs* was published in 1905. Though much more work on early bush and other songs has been done since, The Banjo's still remains a valuable collection. In his introduction he made a valuable point:

> It is hard to believe that among us still are men who can remember the days when convicts in irons tramped the streets of Sydney, and it was unsafe to go to and from Sydney and Parramatta without an armed escort; who were partakers of the roaring days of the diggings, when miners lit their pipes with five-pound notes and shod their horses with gold; who have exchanged shots with Gilbert and Morgan, and have watched the lumbering police of the old days scouring the country to

earn the thousand pounds reward on the head of Ben Hall. So far as materials for ballads go, the first sixty or seventy years of our history are equal to about three hundred years of the life of an old and settled nation.

He set out his editorial objective in a Preface:

The object of the present publication is to gather together all the old bush songs that are worth remembering. Apart from other considerations, there are many Australians who will be reminded by these songs of the life of the shearing sheds, the roar of the diggings townships, and the campfires of the overlanders. The diggings are all deep sinking now, the shearing is done by contract, and the cattle are sent by rail to market, while newspapers travel all over Australia; so there will be no more bush ballads composed and sung, as these were composed and sung, as records of the early days of the nation. In their very roughness, in their absolute lack of any mention of home ties or of the domestic affections, they proclaim their genuineness. They were collected from all parts of Australia, and have been patched together by the compiler to the best of his abilities, with the idea of presenting the song as nearly as possible as it was sung ...[74]

Paterson cannot be said to have been a rigorous editor. He included not only traditional, anonymous songs (of which he sometimes altered the words), but others by more or less contemporary writers. The best of them are those which, he said, 'should be heard to an accompaniment of clashing shears when the voice of a shearer rises through the din caused by the rush and bustle of a shearing shed, the scrambling of the sheep in their pens, and the hurry of the pickers-up; or when, on the roads, the cattle are restless on their camp at night and the man on watch, riding round them strikes up "Bold Jack Donahoo" to steady their nerves a little ... Many a mob of wild, pike-horned Queensland cattle, half inclined to stampede, has listened contentedly to the "Wild Colonial Boy" droned out in true bush fashion until daylight began to break and the mob was safe for another day.'

Only one convict song appears in the collection, but there are a number from the earliest years of settlement, including 'The Beautiful Land of Australia':

> Oh, I've seen a lot of girls, my boys, and drunk
>   a lot of beer,
> And I've met with some of both, chaps, as has
>   left me mighty queer;
> But for beer to knock you sideways, and for girls
>   to make you sigh,
> You must camp at Lazy Harry's, on the road to
>   Gundagai.
>
> CHORUS
>
> But we camped at Lazy Harry's, on the road to
>   Gundagai.
> The road to Gundagai! Not five miles from
>   Gundagai!
> Yes, we camped at Lazy Harry's, on the road to
>   Gundagai.
>
> Well, we chucked our blooming swags off, and
>   we walked into the bar,
> And we called for rum-an'-raspb'ry and a
>   shilling-each cigar.
> But the girl that served the pizen, she winked at
>   Bill and I
> And we camped at Lazy Harry's, not five miles
>   from Gundagai.

> But we camped at Lazy Harry's, on the road to
>   Gundagai.
> The road to Gundagai! Not five miles from
>   Gundagai!
> Yes, we camped at Lazy Harry's, on the road to
>   Gundagai.

Then there were songs from the repertoire of the squatters, including 'The Eumerella Shore':

> There's a happy little valley on the Eumerella shore,
> Where I've lingered many happy hours away,
> On my little free selection I have acres by the score,
> Where I unyoke the bullocks from the dray.

CHORUS

> To my bullocks then I say
> No matter where you stray
> You will never be impounded any more;
> For you're running, running, running on the
>   duffer's piece of land,
> Free selected on the Eumerella shore.

> When the moon has climbed the mountains and
>   the stars are shining bright,
> Then we saddle up our horses and away,
> And we yard the squatters' cattle in the darkness
>   of the night,
> And we have the calves all branded by the day.

CHORUS

> Oh, my pretty little calf,
> At the squatter you may laugh,
> For he'll never be your owner any more;
> For you're running, running, running on the
>   duffer's piece of land,
> Free selected on the Eumerella shore.

> *If we find a mob of horses when the paddock*
> *rails are down,*
> *Although before they're never known to stray,*
> *Oh, quickly will we drive them to some distant*
> *inland town,*
> *And sell them into slav'ry far away.*

CHORUS

> *To Jack Robertson we'll say*
> *You've been leading us astray,*
> *And we'll never go a-farming any more;*
> *For it's easier duffing cattle on the little piece of land*
> *Free selected on the Eumerella shore.*

Robertson made the collection the first of a series of 'Commonwealth' editions, selling at one shilling, and it was a great success – setting the precedent for similar collections which have continued to the present day. Paterson was pleased, and perhaps saw the book's success as another reason why he should not have committed himself to an editor's chair for the indefinite future. Quite apart from not being temperamentally suited to the work, he found that for much of the time he was bored by the office routine. In an attempt to fight the tedium, he rather ironically decided to take on the company's weekly paper, *The Town and Country Journal*, and during his three-year tenure of that chair presided over a variety of pages – a women's page, a literary page, theatre news, sport (of course) and gossip.

But he found the job no more inspiring than editing the daily paper; moreover he was continually receiving requests for articles and verses which he had to turn down because of the pressure of the work. He decided he needed to get out of the whole business of editorship and not doing things by half, decided also to get out of Sydney. The claustrophobia of the city having once more caught up with him, he raised the money to buy a quarter share in a property in south-eastern New South Wales, on the Goodradigbee River, a tributary of the Murrumbidgee.

Coodra Vale was a 40,000 acre station near Wee Jasper – still a small village of only about 80 people at the western foot of the Brindabella Ranges, on the backwaters of Burrinjuck Dam. It is 336 kilometres south-west of Sydney and 54 kilometres south-west of Yass along a partially unsealed road, and still is about as inaccessible as it was when Paterson joined with four other men to buy Coodra Vale.

Raising the cash was not all that easy. He was not a rich man as collections of poetry did not in his day, any more than today, make much money, and his salary as an editor was not particularly generous. But he managed to do so by selling his house and the copyrights of all his literary work. In essence he went back to the bush, to a place only thirty kilometres from Brindabella station, where Miles Franklin had been born.

Reminiscing in the *Evening News*, he described Coodra Vale, lyrically:

> As a station proposition it was best avoided; as a homestead there was nothing better. We had eight miles of a trout river, which ran all the year round, clear and cold in summer, a fierce snow-fed torrent in winter. As the sun was setting, the lyre-birds came out of their fastnesses and called to each other across the valley, imitating everything that they had ever heard. Gorgeous lories came and sat in rows on the spouting that ran round the verandah, protesting shrilly when their tails were pulled by the children. Bower birds with an uncanny scent for fruit would come hurrying up from the end of the garden when the housewife started to peel apples, and would sit on the window-sill of the kitchen, looking expectantly into the room.
>
> Part of the run was enclosed by a dingo-proof fence of thirteen wires, with a strand of barbed wire at top and bottom; and outside of this there were about ten thousand acres of

unfenced country, where one could put sheep
when there was any water, and chance the
dingoes coming in from Lobb's Hole.

One winter they came in when there
were a couple of inches of snow on the
ground, and the fiery cross was sent round to
the neighbouring stations; for the presence
of a "dorg" will make the hill people leave all
other work and go after him. We mustered
some eight or ten armed men, and as I rode in
front on a cream-coloured mountain pony I
happened to look round at the overcoated and
armed figures following me through the snow.
  'Where,' I thought, 'have I seen that
picture before!' And then I remembered it.
Napoleon's retreat from Moscow! I, too,
retreated from the mountain Moscow,
fortunately with less loss than Napoleon, and
resumed city life, not without regrets.[75]

His retreat from Sydney accomplished, The Banjo
settled easily and gratefully into the property. As the resident
shareholder of the syndicate, he enjoyed the countryside over
which he could ride for mile after mile, seeing only wild horses
and cattle, wombats and wallaroos, sleeping at night under the
stars with flying squirrels chattering as they played in the gum
trees. Nearer home, he fished for newly available rainbow trout:

Among other rivers, trout fry were liberated
in the Goodradigbee River. Sufficient time
was allowed for them to grow up, and then
the local inhabitants set about catching them.
A few blackfellows, hanging about the river,
used to spend hours fishing for these trout
with cod lines, baited with half a parrot. They
could see the trout jumping, but could not
induce any of them to bite; and the trout,

generally speaking, were voted a complete
washout.

There was a tradition on this part of the
river that a bunyip had once come ashore there
- something like a calf with whiskers. If there
were any truth in the story, it was probably
a seal which had found its way up from the
mouth of the Murray, but the blackfellows
believed that the bunyip was still in the river
and that it was eating all the trout which were
big enough to bite. Otherwise, why couldn't
they catch them?

Then came the tourists from Sydney,
fitted out to beat the band with artificial
flies and spinners: but these people had
little better luck than the blackfellows, for
the river was so full of feed that the trout did
not bother themselves to rise at flies when
they could get the pupae of dragon flies
and other delicacies without any trouble.
Dry-fly purists, and chuck-and-chance-it
fishermen, who lowered their flies down
the rapids, alike had the poorest of luck:
but they held on in the belief that only a
barbarian would use live bait for trout. Then
somebody caught a big haul of trout using
grasshoppers for bait - but the president of
the dry-fly school said that he would sooner
use a fish-trap than a grasshopper.[76]

The Banjo also enjoyed watching the sheering of sheep
herded from the arid parched uplands, to graze in the pastures
by the river. He described his 'boarding-house for sheep' in
'The Mountain Squatter':

Here in my mountain home,
On rugged hills and steep,
I sit and watch you come,
O Riverinia Sheep! ...

Around me where I sit
The wary wombat goes --
A beast of little wit,
But what he knows, he knows.

The very same remark
Applies to me also;
I don't give out a spark,
But what I know, I know.

My brain perhaps would show
No convolutions deep,
But anyhow I know
The way to handle sheep.

These Riverina cracks,
They do not care to ride
The half-inch hanging tracks
Along the mountain side.

Their horses shake with fear
When loosened boulders go
With leaps, like startled deer,
Down to the gulfs below.

Their very dogs will shirk,
And drop their tails in fright
When asked to go and work
A mob that's out of sight.

My little collie pup
Works silently and wide;
You'll see her climbing up
Along the mountain side.

As silent as a fox
You'll see her come and go,
A shadow through the rocks
Where ash and messmate grow.

Then, lost to sight and sound
Behind some rugged steep,
She works her way around
And gathers up the sheep;

And, working wide and shy,
She holds them rounded up.
The cash ain't coined to buy
That little collie pup.

And so I draw a screw
For self and dog and keep
To boundary-ride for you,
O Riverina Sheep!

And, when the autumn rain
Has made the herbage grow,
You travel off again,
And glad - no doubt - to go.

But some are left behind
Around the mountain's spread,
For those we cannot find
We put them down as dead.

So, when we say adieu
And close the boarding job,
I always find a few
Fresh ear-marks in my mob.

And, what with those I sell,
And what with those I keep,
You pay me pretty well,
O Riverina Sheep![77]

If Paterson's intention had been to relax for a while and then turn his mind to earning some money by his pen, it was not fulfilled. The only writing he did at Coodra Vale was a collection of notes for a possible history of Australian horse-racing, with some essays on the nature and physique of racehorses. (It is worth pointing out that he now lived rather closer to Melbourne – easier to get to the cup.) It seems that George Robertson was not averse to the notion – though surely he cannot have thought of it as a money-making venture. In any case it was only completed in very rough form and left unpublished in any form until the 1960s. No, The Banjo's time at Coodra Vale was almost entirely given up to recreation and we might guess that he needed it. He had never shrunk from hard work, and his editorial and other work seems to have driven him close to a breakdown.

There was one sad excursion from Coodra Vale when Paterson went to Sydney to attend the funeral of his aunt Emily, who died at Gladesville at the age of 91. She had been a remarkable woman, reconciled to her early hardships, and had enjoyed the more intellectually satisfying life she had been able to live in Sydney. Apart from her lifelong interest in literature and languages, she had been all her life a writer of verses, in the manner of many Victorian ladies in far-off England. In Sydney she had been able to indulge the luxury of having some of them printed for distribution to her friends. There too, she had been able to hold soirées for those friends, where verses would be read, music played and sung, and the art of conversation celebrated.

Paterson always kept his emotions to himself and he wrote virtually nothing of his feelings. But he must surely have felt his Aunt Emily's death keenly, as her company alone had done much to make him what he was. There was a second death as Emily's sister Eliza then died, in her ninetieth year. It was not that she had played any major part in The Banjo's life, but it was another link with the past, severed.

What was more or less an exile in Coodra Vale, ended in 1911, but the family did not immediately move back to Sydney. They moved first to a farm called Glen Esk, south of

Grenfell, once a rich gold-mining town, now concentrated on wheat cultivation, and served since 1901 by the railway, which was a convenience. The family was only at Glen Esk for just over a year – time to mark the fact with a single set of verses, 'Song of the Wheat':

> *Furrow by furrow, and fold by fold,*
> *The soil is turned on the plain;*
> *Better than silver and better than gold*
> *Is the surface-mine of the grain.*
> *Better than cattle and better than sheep*
> *In the fight with drought and heat;*
> *For a streak of stubbornness, wide and deep,*
> *Lies hid in a grain of Wheat ...*
>
> *Green and amber and gold it grows*
> *When the sun sinks late in the West;*
> *And the breeze sweeps over the rippling rows*
> *Where the quail and the skylark nest.*
> *Mountain or river or shining star,*
> *There's never a sight can beat --*
> *Away to the sky-line stretching far --*
> *A sea of the ripening Wheat.*[78]

These were almost his final words on country living. He was ready to return to Sydney.

SEVEN

Again to War

So little is known of Paterson's life during the next few years that it seems safe to conclude that it was pretty dull. He clearly hoped to go on being a prominent contributor to the Sydney newspapers, but either because he could not suggest sufficiently interesting topics or because the editors, in the way of editors, had found other people to promote, his name appeared extremely rarely in newsprint.

His income must have been small, and how he managed to support himself and his family is difficult to guess. No doubt there was an income of sorts from his books of verse, but his novel had fallen out of print, to no-one's regret except surely his own. He only truly came to life again, and into the public domain, when Australia was embroiled willy-nilly, in the First World War declared between England and Germany on 4 August 1914. On the following day Australian Prime Minister Sir Joseph Cook declared that 'if the Armageddon is to come, then you and I shall be in it ... If the old country is at war, so are we.' He immediately offered an expeditionary force of 20,000 men, to sail for Europe as soon as shipping could be arranged, and the leader of the opposition, Andrew Fisher, gave unqualified support: Australia would defend Britain 'to the last man and the last shilling.'

By 3 December, Australian troops were disembarking at Alexandria. It had taken only ten days to recruit the 20,000 – indeed over 50,000 had volunteered. It would have been surprising if Paterson hadn't seen the outbreak of hostilities as a great opportunity to renew his journalistic career. At almost fifty he was of course too old to fight, but he immediately went down to the *Sydney Morning Herald* office and volunteered himself as a war correspondent. He found there was something of a problem as the government had decided that it would itself, appoint war correspondents, rather than allow newspapers to select their own.

Paterson thought again, and pressing home his qualification as a man who knew all that there was to be known about horses, contrived to get himself appointed honorary veterinarian to a batch of horses being shipped to Egypt; the *Herald* naturally assured him that they would be delighted to publish any reports he might care to send back to them. They announced him as their 'Special Commissioner in Europe' — and the government, which must have been aware of the subterfuge, apparently accepted this — though reserving the right to deny him the privileges accorded to their own reporters.

Paterson wasted no time. His first article appeared while the expeditionary force — the Australian Imperial Force - was still being recruited. 'Making an Army' described how the recruiting was managed, and the strict medical examination of each recruit. He watched as the men poured into the recruiting offices from city offices and country farms, only for many of them to be rejected as 'unfit for service'. The high standard set for enlistment passed only the fittest men.

He welcomed the fact that the Australians were to be highly paid compared with the British 'Tommies' — six shillings a day rather than the Englishmen's one shilling. This applied also to the many British immigrants who enlisted — some of them, he noticed, ex-servicemen 'wearing as many medals as prize-bulls'. He examined the uniforms of dull khaki wool, the wide-brimmed hats pinned up at one side. He even approved the underclothes — two sets of everything.

On 1 November HMAS *Melbourne* and *Sydney* accompanied 30,000 troops loaded into transport ships out of the harbour and away to war. After the excitement of the departure which, Paterson wrote, provided 'the most wonderful sight that an Australian ever saw', life on board the *Euripides* was rather dull, as he sadly scribbled in his diary on 3 November: 'Sacred Day: Melbourne Cup. Not much chance of hearing what won.' He did his best to see that the horses were comfortable and with the 1899 experience in mind, provided slings so that they could not fall down.

Otherwise there was not much to do and he shared the boredom of the men which was alleviated by the ration of a pint of beer a day. Later, on 9 November, there was the news of the sinking by the *Sydney* of the German battleship *Emden* at North Keeling Island, an atoll in the Indian Ocean about halfway between Australia and Sri Lanka. The British Admiralty gave directions that 'all honours of war are to be accorded to the survivors of the *Emden*, and that the Captain and Officers will not be deprived of their swords', and the First Lord of the Admiralty, Winston Churchill, signalled the *Sydney*: 'Warmest congratulations on the brilliant entry of the Australian Navy into the war, and the signal service rendered to the Allied cause and to peaceful commerce by the destruction of the *Emden*.'

Colombo harbour, when they arrived, was crowded with shipping – Japanese, Russian, English and Australian warships, transports, merchantmen – 'and best of all, alongside the long breakwater the four funnels – the two centre funnels with white streaks round them – of the *Sydney*. It sort of wakes us up to the idea that we have a country,' wrote The Banjo.[79]

In Colombo, Paterson had an enviable scoop: Second Lieutenant Jack Massie, a former international cricketer with whom he had struck up a friendship on board, turned out to be familiar with Capt. John Glossop, the commander of the *Sydney* and introduced the two men. So Paterson was able to get an incontrovertible first-hand description of the engagement with the Emden, which he turned into a dramatic description of the action. On board *Sydney*:

> one shell burst in the after-control, a space of the deck from which the gunfire is controlled. The shell wounded all the men in the control ... The other shell landed in the forward control, and passed over the shoulder of Gunnery-Lieutenant Rahilly, knocking his cap off. It then struck and disabled the range-finder, an instrument about 12 feet long worked in the control, and killed the man working it. It then bounced off the deck, and went overboard without exploding. If it had exploded the

captain and the navigating-lieutenant, who
were in the control, would almost certainly
have been killed ... There was a boy of about
sixteen in the control working a telescope.
When the shell landed he was stunned by the
concussion and was lying under the body of
the man that was killed. As soon as he came to
himself he threw the man's body off him and
started looking for his telescope. 'Where's my
bloody telescope?' was all he said. That's the
Australian Navy for you ...

The two vessels steamed alongside
each other, or rather parallel to each other,
exchanging broadsides at 10,000 yards range.
The first salvo fired by the Sydney appeared
to go right clear over the Emden, but the
Germans said afterwards that the first salvo
landed on them. One shell burst in the poop,
and killed several people, and destroyed her
steering gear. She steered afterwards by means
of the propeller, which reduced her speed
greatly. In any event the Sydney was very
much faster than was the Emden and kept
slightly in the lead, pounding away at her.

The master of the Emden ran her aground on
North Keeling,

on fire in several places, her funnels and one
mast shot away, her decks a shambles, the
captain stupefied by lyddite fumes,[80] and
every man above decks in such a state of
stupefaction through the appalling slaughter,
the din of the explosions and the lyddite
fumes, that no one had presence of mind to
haul down the German flag, which still flew
on her remaining mast ... She was a shambles.
Blood, guts, flesh, and uniforms were all

scattered about. One of our shells had landed behind a gun shield, and had blown the whole gun-crew into one pulp. You couldn't even tell how many men there had been. They must have had forty minutes of hell on that ship, for out of four hundred men a hundred and forty were killed and eighty wounded. And the survivors were practically madmen.[81]

On 1 December the Australian convoy reached the Suez canal, and the rumour went about that the final destination was not to be England, but Egypt. Indeed disembarkation took place at Alexandria, where Paterson was released from the tenuous duties he had had as a vet. He decided to make for London, where he hoped it would be easier to get accreditation as a war correspondent. His hope was in vain. When he went to the War Office on 14 December, he 'found the waiting-rooms and passages absolutely blocked by old generals, old colonels, young and old civilians, who all want to do something or give something – and they want to get to the front. I want to get to the front myself.'

One contact he had in London was the Agent-General for New South Wales, Sir Timothy Coghlan, who he had known in Sydney. Coghlan offered to get him to France as an ambulance-driver attached to Lady Dudley's Hospital. Lady Dudley, a Quaker, was the estranged wife of the second Earl of Dudley, a former Governor-General of Australia. He was to command a Yeomanry unit in Egypt and Gallipoli, and Lady Dudley set up a hospital for Australians and clubs for officers in northern France. (In 1918 Lady Dudley was appointed a C.B.E and Royal Red Cross for her war services.) Her hospital at Wimereux, 8 kilometres from Boulogne-sur-Mer on the coast, was already famous even in the first months of the war. It was so well established and staffed that wounded men, Australian or not, automatically asked to be sent there. Paterson accepted Coghlan's offer immediately – especially since he heard that the hospital was actually run by a Colonel William Eames, who he had met in South Africa.

While waiting for the arrangements to be made, he took a brief holiday in Ireland, visiting the famous Straffon Stud near Dublin, eager to find just how the Irish bred such good horses. The process remained a mystery – the success of Kennedy, the stud's owner, seemed largely to rely on instinct, though the man himself credited the soil and the climate.

The Banjo was naturally delighted to accept an invitation to ride with a local hunt. He distinguished himself by accidentally knocking another man and his horse into a ditch and was rebuked by the Master: 'You jumped on a man, did you,' he roared. 'Just because we're poor Irish, you think you can come all the way from Australia and jump on us! In the Shires they'd stand you up against a wall and shoot you! But I'll tell you what I'll do. There's a lot of these lads here haven't paid their subscriptions. I'll point em out to you, and you can come along and jump on em to your heart's content.' Later The Banjo told the head groom about the incident. 'Ye done well,' the man said – 'they'd have felt hurted if an Australian hadn't done something square for em'.[82]

Paterson arrived at Wimereux on 23 December, and was immediately told off to drive one of the ambulances ferrying wounded over the rough, cobbled roads from Boulogne station to the hospital, which had been established in a large chateaux with a golf-course attached. It was staffed almost entirely by Australians, several of whom he knew – Eames, of course, but also a Dr McCormick, who he remembered from South Africa, and a surgeon from Sydney, Herschell Harris, who presided over what was at that time the only x-ray machine anywhere near the Front.

The English nurses had clearly come under the influence of their Australian superiors – especially McCormick, who had a colourful vocabulary. One visiting officer told The Banjo that when a young and inexperienced doctor had arrived from England and attempted to interfere with the treatment of a patient, 'two girls turned on him, and gave him a cursing that would have taken away the breath of a drill sergeant.' When the doctor reported them to Eames, the latter simply remarked, 'But, my dear fellow, those are McCormick's two nurses! All

McCormick's nurses swear. Nobody objects to it – they always do it.'[83]

Lady Dudley herself descended on the hospital from time to time and her visits were greeted with some irritation by the staff. She was determined, without any training, to be a nurse, and her ministrations consisted of parading around the wards dressed in white followed by an orderly carrying a bucket of water, stopping at every bed to wash 'the dear faces' of the wounded, even if they were breathing their last.

Paterson undoubtedly did useful work at Wimereux, but he had only accepted the position as an excuse to get to France, where he hoped to be able in some way to see action. This hope was more and more obviously in vain and now he heard that military action was almost certainly soon to accelerate in Egypt. A desert campaign meant that horses would be in demand, and he decided to return to Australia, where he could surely be useful in obtaining and training them.

Back in Sydney in July 1915, he applied for a commission in the Australian Military Forces, and had no difficulty in obtaining it. On 13 October he was gazetted as a lieutenant, and almost immediately sent to Maribyrnong, in Victoria, given the rank of Captain, and assigned to one of the ten squadrons in two First Australian Remount units. He found himself amid a motley crowd of men who looked, he later said, like 'Australia's last hope'. They included jockeys, elderly grooms, horse-breakers from the bush, men who had earned their living riding rough in fairground shows, gentlemen polo-players and drovers - but they all had in common the fact that they were fine horsemen. He embarked with the units on 12 November to become part of the Remount Service in Egypt, leaving his wife, Grace and Hugh behind in a house in Cooper Street, Edgecliff. In due course, Alice Paterson was herself to travel to the Middle East to serve as a nurse the children left with their grandmother.

Before he went, The Banjo wrote a set of verses, an 'open letter to the troops' full of national pride:

From shearing shed and cattle run
From Broome to Hobson's Bay,
Each native-born Australian son
Stands straighter up today.

The man who used to 'hump his drum'
On far-out Queensland runs
Is fighting side by side with some
Tasmanian farmers' sons.

The fisher-boys dropped sail and oar
To grimly stand the test
Along that storm-swept Turkish shore
With miners from the west.

The old state jealousies of yore
Are dead as Pharaoh's sow,
We're not State children any more —
We're all Australians now!

Paterson and the other members of the remount units disembarked at Port Said on 8 December, and established a depot literally in the shadow of the pyramids at Mahdi al Khabiri, now a suburb of Cairo. There he and his companions got down to work. In *Happy Dispatches*[84] Paterson explains that:

> the work of the Remount Depot is to take over the rough uncivilised horses that are bought all over the world by army buyers; to quieten them and condition them and get them accustomed to being heel-roped; and finally to issue them in such a state of efficiency that a heavily-accoutred trooper can get on and off them under fire if need be. We had fifty thousand horses and about ten thousand mules through the depot, in lots of [a] thousand at a time. All these horses and mules had to be fed three times and watered twice every day; groomed thoroughly; the

manure carted away and burnt, and each animal had to be exercised everyday including Sundays and holidays.

The Banjo by no means despised the mule, an extremely useful animal. As he pointed out in one of the few sets of verses he wrote during the war:

> ... *if you go where the depots are as the dawn is*
> *   breaking grey,*
> *By the waning light of the morning star as the*
> *   dust cloud clears away,*
> *You'll see a vision among the dust like a man*
> *   and a mule combined --*
> *It's the kind of thing you must take on trust for*
> *   its outlines aren't defined,*
> *A thing that whirls like a spinning top and*
> *   props like a three legged stool,*
> *And you find its a long-legged Queensland boy*
> *   convincing an Army mule.*
> *And the rider sticks to the hybrid's hide like*
> *   paper sticks to a wall,*
> *For a 'magnoon' Waler is next to ride with*
> *   every chance of a fall,*
> *It's a rough-house game and a thankless game,*
> *   and it isn't a game for a fool,*
> *For an army's fate and a nation's fame may*
> *   turn on an Army mule.*
> *And if you go to the front-line camp where the*
> *   sleepless outposts lie,*
> *At the dead of night you can hear the tramp of*
> *   the mule train toiling by.*
> *The rattle and clink of a leading-chain, the*
> *   creak of the lurching load,*
> *As the patient, plodding creatures strain at their*
> *   task in the shell-torn road,*
> *Through the dark and the dust you may watch*
> *   them go till the dawn is grey in the sky,*

And only the watchful pickets know when the
'All-night Corps' goes by.
And far away as the silence falls when the last of
the train has gone,
A weary voice through the darkness: 'Get on
there, men, get on!'
It isn't a hero, built to plan, turned out by the
modern schools,
It's only the Army Service man a-driving his
Army mules.[85]

What with horses and mules, the motley crowd of rough-riders clearly had their work cut out, and it is certainly the case that, as a visiting general remarked, the pyramids had never seen anything like it in forty centuries. Paterson's description of the scene should be left alone as a vivid piece of reporting:

> The rough-riders had come out carrying their saddles and dressed for action. Field service uniform for a rough-rider consists of a shirt and riding-breeches; no leggings or puttees, and their socks were pulled up outside the ends of their breeches. They wore elastic-sided boots specially made in Australia, with smooth tops so that there would be nothing to catch the rider's foot in the stirrup. Their saddles, also specially made, had high pommels and cantles with big knee and thigh-pads. Dust rose in clouds from the quiet horses going out to exercise; and as for the flies – there are five elements in Egypt: earth, air, flies, fire, and water, in the order of seniority.
>
> Sergeant-Major Dempsey, a six-foot-two Australian, straight as a stringy-bark sapling and equally as tough, took charge of the rough-riding. He had not yet acquired the military method of command. He said:

'Now, you, Bill, get hold of that bay horse,' instead of barking out orders as a sergeant-major should. Men do not get on rough horses by word of command, they get on when they can.

'Charley, you take that big chestnut fellow. George, you take that black horse with the Battle Abbey brand. We'll rub some stickfast on your saddle, for they'll all buck. I was breakin' in there once, and I never struck such a lot of snakes in me life.'

Having allotted the worst-looking horses to the best riders, the sergeant-major says, 'Now, boys, grab your horses. Get to 'em.' There is a charming lack of formality about the proceedings. One rider begins to croon a song:

'Tis of a brave old squatter, boys, his name was
William Binn.
He had two gallant sons was known both near
and far,
He had some outlaw horses and none could
break them in.
So I went down, rough-riding, on old
Bulginbar.

'Tiger' Richards, a strapping young horse-breaker from the Riverina, says:

'This is my lucky day: look what I've got.' And he drags out a sleepy old bay horse that looks more like a ration-carrier's hack than an outlaw. But Dempsey is seldom wrong. As soon as the old horse sees the saddle he tries to pull away and drags Tiger and the saddle all over the compound.

'Come on, you silly Queensland cow,' says the Tiger. Do you think I'm an alligator?'

'Watch him, Tiger,' says Dempsey. 'That cove threw Billy Waite' (a celebrated rider) 'in our show in Queensland.'

'He's struck something better than Billy Waite this time, then. Hit him over the rump so I can get him in a corner and have a few words with him.'

In a moment the compound was full of trouble. Horses were bucking all over the place. A big chestnut horse, as soon as he was mounted, threw himself straight over backwards and narrowly missed pinning his rider to the ground.

A waspish little bay mare refused to move at all when mounted, and crouched right down till her chest nearly touched the ground. It appeared that she was going to roll over, and her rider kicked his feet out of the stirrups. As he did so, she unleashed a terrific spring that shot him out of the saddle and sent him soaring in the air, high enough to see over the Pyramids – or at any rate so he said. Some unmounted brutes bolted back into the compound and fell over the ropes, while others set sail out into the desert as though they were going back to Australia.[86]

That Paterson was extremely efficient, is attested by his promotion in October to the rank of Major with the British Expeditionary Force, working now at Moascar, near Ismailia on the main route from Egypt to Palestine. There, he was encountered by Kermit Roosevelt, the son of the former American President 'Teddy' Roosevelt, who had been commissioned in the British army and served in Mesopotamia.

Roosevelt had been given a copy of *The Man from Snowy River* as a boy, and was delighted to meet Major 'Banjo' Paterson, 'a man of about sixty, with long moustaches and strong aquiline features ... He has lived everything that he has written. At different periods of his life he has dived for pearls in the islands, herded sheep, broken broncos, and known every chance and change of Australian station life. The Australians told me that when he was in his prime he was regarded as the best rider in Australia. A recent feat about which I heard much mention was when he drove 300 mules straight through Cairo without losing a single animal, conclusively proving his argument against those who had contested that such a thing could not be done.'[87]

The Australians, Paterson included, welcomed the appointment of General Edmund Allenby to command their forces: they trusted him, and Paterson in particular had met him in South Africa and had added confidence in the new commander. Allenby remembered him, and greeted him personally – but rather upset him by criticising his Australian horses as 'a common hairy-legged lot.' Paterson pointed out that the reason they were not as superb as the Australian Lancers' horses that had served in South Africa was that there were simply not enough good beasts available. If he was somewhat short with the irascible General it was no doubt because he himself was exhausted by over-work. Indeed shortly afterwards he was hospitalised for a month before returning to work and as horsemaster readying a detachment of hundreds of saddle horses and mules for transfer from Moascar to Rafa. These travelled by rail as far as Kantara and were then driven on to Rafa.

There is little doubt that Paterson longed to see action – but while the British 4th cavalry together with the Australian and New Zealand Mounted Division drove the Turks away from Jerusalem, and gathered in the valley of the Jordan ready to advance towards Nazareth, he remained stuck in Moascar, still breaking in horses to send forward.

Gradually, life became easier as the victory of the allies made the need for fresh mounts less vital, and finding himself with time on his hands Paterson began to organise displays of rough-riding which captivated the Egyptian aristocracy. Sometimes these consisted of hotly contested trials between Australian and British troops. His squadron won five out of seven open events at one show, including one for wrestling on horseback, when 'one of my Queenslanders, a big half caste named Ned Kelly, pulled the English tommies off their horses like picking apples off a tree.'

These jollifications were not without cost: at one time Paterson's group lost two men with broken legs, one with a fractured shoulder-blade, two with badly crushed ankles, and about seven others disabled in one way or another.

On 31 October the Turks signed an armistice – eleven days before the German capitulation in France. It was time to go home. Not, however, for the horses. The Australian Government was unwilling to spare the money to repatriate them, making the general excuse of difficulties with quarantine. Thousands were sold to the Indian Army, but against public opinion and protests from the RSPCA, 20,000 Australian horses who had fought in the Desert Campaign were sold to the Egyptians. The troopers had seen how harshly the natives treated their animals, and the thought of the horses becoming slaves in a rock quarry or being whipped on the streets of Cairo was not an option. Many were taken to the desert and shot, officially or otherwise. This sickened Paterson so much that he became ill, and was forcibly sent on a fortnight's sick leave.

Alice Paterson's presence in Egypt helped her husband to secure an early passage home; they sailed together on the *Kildonian Castle*, his army service officially ending on 2 July 1919. The Banjo came home with a few medals – one for his brief service at Lady Dudley's hospital, the ordinary silver British War Medal and the Victory Medal that, as it were, had come up with the rations. But despite his invaluable service in organising the supply of horses to the troops in Egypt, it is very doubtful that he was personally satisfied with his war service. Though he must have realised from the start that he would never become an active fighting soldier, his ambition to be a war reporter had died hard, and he may never have fully got over the disappointment of not achieving that goal.

EIGHT

The Final Years

Paterson and Alice took a house in New South Head Road, Woollahra. And now, what was to be done? How was he to earn a living? A new collection of verses – *Saltbush Bill, J.P., and other verses*, had been published in 1917, but had contained little new work, and was generally regarded as unsatisfactory, though the character of Saltbush Bill himself caught on to a certain extent. In the same year George Robertson had issued *Three Elephant Power and other stories*, which had only just paid for the cost of publication. Robertson kept encouraging Paterson to write more humorous verse, but he seemed incapable of doing so – perhaps the arduous work of the war years had simply exhausted him, or perhaps his Muse had simply withered and died. In 1921 the publisher brought out Collected Verse, which over the next few years, sold just sufficient copies to justify keeping it in print. But to all intents and purposes, Paterson's career as a poet was over.

Was there some hope in fiction? On the voyage home from the war, he had written a short novel, *The Cook's Dog*. It was a romance between a young Australian called (unlikely though it perhaps sounds) Gilbert Farquarson ('a tall, loosely-made, good-natured young Hercules') and slim, brown-eyed Ellen Macalister of Brawbucketty, in Scotland. It is fair to say that the manuscript was a total disaster. The Banjo himself, when he read it through, thought it was stiff and he would have to 'do it over'. Robertson assured him that he would never make anything of it as it had hardly one redeeming feature, and it wouldn't be improved even if he re-wrote it 'till hell's blue'.

He did however still have his talent as a journalist, and when in 1919 a former colleague of his, Claude McKay, launched a new weekly newspaper, *Smith's Weekly* (the title commemorating its major supporter, Sydney's Lord Mayor Sir Joynton Smith), Paterson was among the first writers to be asked to contribute. He chose for his first article to write about Harry Hawker, the Australian pilot who combined serious attempts at record flights with flying displays. He wrote several more, but upon the death of an old friend, J. F. Archibald, who had been the paper's literary editor, Paterson was dropped after only five months' work.

He moved on to a paper in which he was much more at home – *The Sportsman*. Established twenty years, it was in need of an editor, and Paterson was the obvious man for the job. Though the paper covered all sport - Paterson contributed articles on boxing, swimming, sailing and cricket and renewed his youthful interest in skulling - his main preoccupation remained horse racing. He became more than ever a familiar figure at Flemington and Randwick, with his old outsize binoculars, happily chatting with jockeys and owners.

This is perhaps the place to look a little more closely at his lifelong love of, and one might say addiction to, the horse – to breeding, riding and racing. He seems at one stage to have owned a race-horse, and according to the artist Norman Lindsay, lost money on it. He may also at one time have owned and trained jumpers. He certainly knew and learned over his lifetime, almost everything there was to be known about horses, and if his novel *The Shearer's Colt* failed to succeed as a novel, the descriptions of races and the horses involved are vivid and completely believable. Take for instance his portrait of the colt, Sensation:

> Dark chestnut in colour, with a long, narrow blaze down his face, Sensation strode out on to the grass with the easy stride of a panther. It seemed strange that so massive a creature could move so daintily. His silky tapering ears and his steel-like legs told of a throwback to his Arab ancestry, while his size was evidently an inheritance from the other blood – possibly Spanish – that goes to make up the thoroughbred. His head was set at an obtuse angle, throwing his nostrils forward, and the width of his gullet left room, as his trainer said, for a bird to build its nest between his jaws. His neck was only slightly arched, and

appeared light for so big a horse, but the arch
and the solidity would come later on in life.
He presented a sort of streamline effect, for
his neck ran back into his shoulders, and
his shoulders ran back into his ribs, with a
smoothness that made it hard to say where
the one ended and the other began. A deep,
but by no means broad, chest was another
streamline feature. And he had no suspicion
of a 'waist', for his ribs ran back to a slightly
arched loin which gave the impression of the
strength and suppleness of a steel spring. His
hips were broad and his rump was carried
back for an appreciable distance without any
droop – much as one sees it in the old picture
of Stockwell taken in the days when the
thoroughbreds were closer to the Arab type
than they are today.[88]

The problem is that, as in all his fiction, Paterson's
characterisation of horses is far better than his characterisation
of his speople.

He spent some time on his book about *Racehorses and
Racing*, most of which he had written in Coodra Vale and
which he worked on again in his retirement, but it was never
published in his lifetime. In it he dealt with a great range of
topics, including the stud-book, buying horses and training
them, racing and its practices, jockeys, tipsters and bookies. He
described any number of the characters who lived for racing
and spent their time mostly at racecourses, and he forecast a
great future for Australian horses provided that wise breeding
made use of the best European sires for sturdy native mares.

As a rider, he had been remarkable – particularly
considering the weakness in his right arm and hand. Apart
from his prowess at polo, he was an ardent steeple-chaser and
won prizes at both sports. His love of racing, born so long ago
at Bogolong, was life-long. But anything which could be done
on a horse which involved skilful riding and the excitement

of controlling a horse under difficult circumstances, appealed to him. In the Northern Territory, for instance, he got a taste for buffalo hunting. The buffalos were originally brought from Timor to the Northern Territory in the 1820s, and abandoned so that they ran wild and bred astonishingly quickly and prolifically. They were hunted for their profitable hides, the hunters controlling their horses with one hand and carrying a rifle in the other with which to shoot the buffalo as it and the horse raced side by side. If this was a sport, it was a dangerous one – half a dozen bullets could fail to stop a buffalo which even badly wounded, would turn and charge. The trick was to shoot into the loins, paralysing the beast, but while racing at speed this took great skill.

Paterson wrote about the hunt in the *Sydney Mail*, contrasting his own performance with that of a professional hunter:

> There is a whiz and a rush of hooves, and one of the professional shooters, sitting square in his saddle, dashes past the novice, shaves a palm tree or two by a hair's breadth, and swoops down on the buffalo like a hawk on a pigeon. He has no trouble in managing his rifle and his horse, recognising the urgency of the case, brings him alongside the quarry in two or three bounds. The buffalo swerves at once, but the trained horse follows his every movement. The shooter leans forward holding out his rifle, elbow up and muzzle down, exactly like a man going to spear pig. Bang! goes the carbine, and through the jet of white smoke the novice sees the buffalo sink to the ground paralysed, shot through the loins, while the horse swings clear of his falling victim, and 'I'm sorry to rob you of him, mister,' says the shooter apologetically, 'but he would have got away in those palms.' The novice swallowed his mortification, and asks how the two men got on. 'Shot every one

of the mob,' is the answer. And, sure enough,
outside the palms lie all the rest of the herd,
still kicking in the agonies of death.[89]

The writer one thinks of when reading The Banjo's
excited descriptions of blood sports is Ernest Hemingway,
who had a similar interest in describing the deaths of
creatures he had killed, or of the bulls he watched others
kill. It is not perhaps a lovable trait in Paterson, but he was a
man of his time. What can be said is that his prose is virile,
specific, and memorable.

It was just as he took over the editorship of *The
Sportsman* that news came of the death of his old friend and
sparring partner Henry Lawson, who was given a State funeral
in St. Andrew's Cathedral. Paterson did not attend and though
almost every Australian newspaper – from as far afield as
Brisbane – was represented, *The Sportsman* was not. There is little
point in speculating about the reason; sympathetic writers have
suggested that because the funeral was on a Monday, it would
have been impossible for the editor of a sporting newspaper to
attend. This is of course nonsense. Was there a whiff of jealousy
in the air? Did Paterson realise that Lawson had been a better
poet than he, and foresee that his own funeral would probably
be a much lower-key event? It seems possible – even probable.

His salary as editor was eventually bolstered by fees as
a director of the company which published it. He joined the
board in 1925 and for the first time for some years (apart from
his war service), he had a secure income. He contributed little
of his own to the paper, sometimes using verse to advance his
firm support of the 'white Australia' policy and his dislike of the
Chinese who worked in the northern territories. An example is
in 'A Job for McGuinness', about a labourer who could not find
work until:

> ... *perhaps - later on - when the Chow and the Jap*
> *Begin to drift down from the tropics,*
> *When a big yellow stain spreading over the map*
> *Provides some disquieting topics,*

> *Oh, it's then when they're wanting a man that*
> *will stand*
> *In the trench where his own kith and kin is,*
> *With a frown on his face and a gun in his hand --*
> *Then there might be a job for McGuinness!* [90]

Occasionally he scribbled down a piece of verse just because he could. For instance when he became irritated by the continual 'literals' (printers') mistakes in the columns of his paper:

> *The Editor wrote his political screed*
> *In ink that was fainter and fainter;*
> *He rose to the call of his country's need,*
> *And in spiderish characters wrote with speed,*
> *A column on 'Cutting the Painter'.*
>
> *The 'reader' sat in his high-backed chair,*
> *For literals he was a hunter;*
> *But he stared aghast at the column long*
> *Of the editorial hot and strong,*
> *For the comp. inspired by some sense of wrong*
> *Had headed it 'Gutting the Punter'.* [91]

Paterson remained at the helm of *the Sportsman* until 1930, when on his 66th birthday he was bound to retire. Reading the recollections of some of the men who worked with and for him, one wonders whether retirement meant much of a change for him. For some years he had taken to attending the office only in the mornings, usually spending the afternoons at the Australian Club talking with friends, perhaps enjoying a game of cards, or simply dozing in a comfortable chair.

George Robertson perhaps saw Paterson's enforced idleness as an opportunity to persuade him to return to poetry. The *Collected Poems*, though not a sensational success, had nevertheless sold steadily over the years, and he now began to encourage the author to return to the light verse which the publisher believed was his strongest suit. He even sent Paterson a cheque for a hundred pounds as an advance on a possible poem along the lines of the extremely successful 'Sentimental Bloke' by C. J. Dennis, which had been published in 1916 and sold 65,000 copies in its first year. But Paterson returned the cheque; he felt 'too flat' he said, to attempt the task. All he felt capable of was occasional journalism.

The problem was that no-one wanted his writing. It had been so long since the success of *The Man from Snowy River* that both readers and editors seemed to think he must be dead. But a surprising new means of augmenting his annuity came in 1931, when he approached the Australian Broadcasting Company to ask whether they might be interested in broadcasting occasional 'essays'.

The Company had been set up by various theatre owners and others in the entertainment business, to supply programmes to various radio stations – in Sydney, to 2FC and 2BL. It was glad to employ Paterson, who read some of his verse and also contributed talks, one for instance to publicise the Archibald Prize, recently established by J. F. Archibald, the founder of *The Bulletin*. His most successful talk however was about his time in South Africa, in particular about the remarkable Dr Tom Fiaschi. He clearly had a good microphone personality, and a rather slow, distinctly Australian voice which he used to advantage in the anecdotes he told. A later talk about Australian literature virtually invented the idea that Australia suffered from an inferiority complex. Other talks followed – for instance about life in the goldfields of Western Australia and on 'Australian men and horses' - all for a fee of five guineas each.

Broadcasting however did not offer regular opportunities, and though Paterson made various suggestions for quite elaborate series of broadcasts, none were accepted. (It was perhaps because, as one ABC man said, 'most people believe he is dead, along with Milton, Keats and all the rest of them.') Nor did the occasional talk really repay profitably the amount of time spent in writing the scripts – hammered out now by two fingers on a typewriter Paterson had bought, his handwriting having become too shaky to be easily read.

In all the circumstances, he was pleased to receive a commission to write a book for children. It came from a somewhat eccentric new publisher, Jack Lindsay, a son of the artist Norman Lindsay. Jack had been in Europe where, with another Australian, P.R. Stephenson, he had been running an underground press, publishing obscene books. Returning home, he persuaded the company which now owned *The Bulletin*, to set up Endeavour Press to publish books by Australian authors, and invited Paterson to write a book for children, to be illustrated by his father. *The Animals Noah Forgot* came out in 1933, went into a second edition in 1934, and then was seen no more.

In some of the poems which made up the collection, Paterson almost regained his form – for instance in his verses about the problems of driving a herd of billy-goats:

> Come all ye lads of the droving days, ye
>   gentlemen unafraid,
> I'll tell you all of the greatest trip that ever a
>   drover made,
> For we rolled our swags, and we packed our
>   bags, and taking our lives in hand,
> We started away with a thousand goats, on the
>   billy-goat overland.
> There wasn't a fence that'd hold the mob, or
>   keep 'em from their desires;
> They skipped along the top of the posts and
>   cake-walked on the wires.
> And where the lanes had been stripped of grass
>   and the paddocks were nice and green,
> The goats they travelled outside the lanes and
>   we rode in between.
> The squatters started to drive them back, but
>   that was no good at all,
> Their horses ran for the lick of their lives from
>   the scent that was like a wall:
> And never a dog had pluck or gall in front of
>   the mob to stand
> And face the charge of a thousand goats on the
>   billy-goat overland.

We found we were hundreds over strength when
we counted out the mob;
And they put us in jail for a crowd of thieves
that travelled to steal and rob:
For every goat between here and Bourke, when
he scented our spicy band,
Had left his home and his work to join in the
billy-goat overland.

Then there was 'A Dog's Mistake':

He had drifted in among us as a straw drifts
with the tide,
He was just a wand'ring mongrel from the
weary world outside;
He was not aristocratic, being mostly ribs and hair,
With a hint of spaniel parents and a touch of
native bear.
He was very poor and humble and content with
what he got,
So we fed him bones and biscuits, till he
heartened up a lot;
Then he growled and grew aggressive, treating
orders with disdain,
Till at last he bit the butcher, which would
argue want of brain.

Now the butcher, noble fellow, was a sport
beyond belief,
And instead of bringing actions he brought half
a shin of beef,
Which he handed on to Fido, who received it as a right
And removed it to the garden, where he
buried it at night.
'Twas the means of his undoing, for my wife,
who'd stood his friend,
To adopt a slang expression, 'went in off the
deepest end',

For among the pinks and pansies, the gloxinias
and the gorse
He had made an excavation like a graveyard for a horse.
Then we held a consultation which decided on his fate:
'Twas in anger more than sorrow that we led
him to the gate,
And we handed him the beef-bone as provision
for the day,
Then we opened wide the portal and we told
him, 'On your way."

There was one more book to come – one which has been invaluable to everyone who has tried to trace the course of Paterson's life. He was persuaded to write his reminiscences by Angus and Robertson. George Robertson was now dead, but his successor was sympathetic to Paterson and believed that enough people remembered his name to make a book of his memories saleable. *Happy Dispatches* came out in 1934, but its reception was another disappointment; the people about whom he wrote were mostly only names to Australian readers – and not names which meant much to them. The book sold poorly and Paterson returned to broadcasting. He sold to the ABC a series of fifteen talks – though they were to be read by an actor, since someone at the ABC had now decided that his voice was 'not suitable' for broadcasting. (Clearly there was some internal politicking about this, for by all accounts he had an excellent microphone presence.)

He covered a wide range of subjects in the talks: the development of the Northern Territory (he believed that modern motor transport would enable the development of a large-scale 'chilled-beef' industry), pearl fishing, the various newspapers of the various states, the discovery of gold in New Guinea, and in particular life in the bush on the western plains. For a number of reasons, which had to do with changes of management and policy at the ABC, with the end of the talks Paterson's career in radio also came to an end. Any talks he gave in future were given privately, to friends, usually at the Australian Club

Paterson was now toying with an idea for another novel – one which he had conceived as long ago as 1902. In *The Shearer's Colt*, Englishman Hilton Fitzroy sent to Australia to make his fortune, joins the Queensland Mounted Police. The story develops into a racing yarn about a marvellous colt, Sensation, which is bought by Red Fred, a wealthy squatter. The colt wins the St. Leger and is taken to England to run in more profitable races. There, a gang attempts to dope the colt and Fitzroy (who has become part of Red Fred's entourage) is injured in a fracas. Meanwhile Red Fred courts the Countess of Fysshe and Fynne, a wealthy widow and ex-chorus-girl. The plot becomes ever more complex and unlikely, but ends with a breathtaking race closely won by Sensation, Fitzroy makes his fortune, Red Fred and the Countess marry, and a happy ending is easily achieved.

Today a good editor might help The Banjo to pull the story together – though it would be a huge task; the descriptions of horses and racing are admirable, but again the characters mere pasteboard. Unfortunately Paterson also lacked both the skill to set the story in contemporary Australia and the ability to write it as a 'period' piece. Though *The Shearer's Colt*, published in 1935, contains some wonderful studies of horses, he even fails to bring to life his old friend Marie Lloyd, thinly described as the Countess of Fysshe and Fynne, formerly chorus-girl Connie Galbraith. The book received few notices and captured few readers.

One interesting episode for the contemporary reader however, is the appearance of a horse whisperer:

> a man who can shut himself in a loose box with a dangerous horse, and he'll begin talking to it and in a little while the horse will follow him about, rubbing its head against him. It's a gift. There used to be plenty of them in England and Ireland. There's a man knocking about here. A worthless sheep-stealing scoundrel he is too, and he has the gift. He can go into a yard with one of my unbroken station colts

and an old mare, and he'll work the old mare up alongside the youngster and talk to it. And while you're expecting to see the colt ram its forefoot down his throat, he has it caught and saddled and he's riding it round the yard. I've known him come here and catch a green unbroken bushy scrubber that had never been fed and handled in its life, and he'd ride it away next day and lead another unbroken horse off its back.[92]

Paterson had always dreaded old age. Thirty or more years ago, he had written a poem which echoed A.E. Housman's 'Loveliest of trees' in *The Shropshire Lad*:

The fields of youth are filled with flowers,
The wine of youth is strong:
What need have we to count the hours?
The summer days are long.

But soon we find to our dismay
That we are drifting down
The barren slopes that fall away
Towards the foothills grim and grey
That lead to Old Man's Town.

And marching with us on the track
Full many friends we find:
We see them looking sadly back
For those who've dropped behind

But God forfend a fate so dread --
Alone to travel down
The dreary road we all must tread,
With faltering steps and whitening head,
The road to Old Man's Town![93]

Happily he had escaped that fate: he was now an old man, but by no means alone, with a wife, a son, two daughters, and now grand-children. Gradually he sank more and more into inactivity. At Christmas 1938 a reminiscent article appeared in the *Sydney Mail* in which he wrote about the genesis of some of his best-known poems, speaking of them as 'rough and unpolished', not claiming immortality, or even much of a right to remembrance for them.

There was a brief blaze of publicity in 1939 when in the King's New Year's honours list Paterson was awarded the C.B.E. The *Sydney Morning Herald* accepted and published five articles in which he reminisced about various aspects and incidents of his life, in a style lively enough to recall his best journalism. Extracts from these articles have been included a few times in this book.

He was now distinctly unwell; he had inherited a weakness of the chest, and his heart had been giving trouble for some time. He found walking difficult, and gradually began to fail, seeming to lose interest in life, making no comment for instance on the outbreak of the Second World War. In February 1941 he was taken to a private hospital at Darling Point, where his situation was not regarded as grave, and he was told he could go home. As he waited for his wife to come and fetch him, his heart stopped. That evening, the evening of 5 February, the author Vance Palmer, a popular broadcaster, paid him a tribute on the ABC. Banjo Paterson, he said, 'laid hold both of our affections and imaginations; he made himself a vital part of the country we all know and love, and it would not only have been a poorer country but one far less united in bonds of intimate feeling, if he had never lived and written'.

NINE
Banjo Paterson's Poetry

How did Banjo Paterson become one of the most recognised and appreciated authors of Australian verse?

His remarkable maternal grandmother, Emily Barton, must in the first place have been largely responsible. When at the age of ten he was sent to Sydney to live with Emily in her home at Gladesville, and eventually to Sydney grammar school, he did not only benefit from his formal school education but from Emily's own love of literature. She had a small (or perhaps not so small) library which included poetry, of which she was fond – she was a good amateur poet herself. The small group of friends she regularly entertained were also literate and sophisticated, and no doubt read as widely as she did.

And what did they read? No doubt the prose-writers of the period were well explored – but as to poetry there was not a great deal of first-rate native work to engage their attention. The first collection of poetry by a native-born Australian had been Charles Tompson's *Wild Notes from the Lyre of a Native Minstrel* (1826), and this and three other poets of the colonial era were very probably on Emily's shelves. Charles Harpur, who published between the 1820s and his death in 1868, wrote most effectively about the Australian landscape, though he also published love poetry and verses about social conditions. But he was no technician; his verse was often clumsy and limping: lines from *A Midsummer Noon in the Australian Forest* are representative:

> *All the birds and insects keep*
> *Where the coolest shadows sleep;*
> *Even the busy ants are found*
> *Resting in their pebbled mound;*
> *Even the locust clingeth now*
> *Silent to the barky bough:*
> *Over hills and over plains*

Quiet, vast and slumbrous, reigns.
Only there's a drowsy humming
From yon warm lagoon slow coming:
'Tis the dragon-hornet—see!
All bedaubed resplendently,
Yellow on a tawny ground—
Each rich spot nor square nor round,
Rudely heart-shaped, as it were
The blurred and hasty impress there
Of a vermeil-crusted seal
Dusted o'er with golden meal . . .

Thomas Henry Kendall (1839-1882) was a not dissimilar case. His verse is often glum and depressive, though when he writes of the Australian landscape he is often better than Harpur, and one of his poems, *Bell Birds*, still finds its place in anthologies:

By channels of coolness the echoes are calling,
And down the dim gorges I hear the creek falling:
It lives in the mountain where moss and the sedges
Touch with their beauty the banks and the ledges.

Through breaks of the cedar and sycamore bowers
Struggles the light that is love to the flowers;
And, softer than slumber, and sweeter than singing,
The notes of the bell-birds are running and ringing . .

English-born Adam Lindsay Gordon (1833-1870) was the best-known of the three – in 2009 a bust was dedicated to him in Poets' Corner of Westminster Abbey, and unlike his two contemporaries his poetry has never entirely fallen from sight or sound. He wrote about the upright manly character of Australia and the rough beauty of its landscape. He was technically both extremely adept and unconsciously tin-eared: both qualities illustrated in *The Swimmer:*

With short, sharp, violent lights made vivid,
To southward far as the sight can roam,
Only the swirl of the surges livid,
The seas that climb and the surfs that comb.
Only the crag and the cliff to nor'ward,
And the rocks receding, and reefs flung forward,
And waifs wreck'd seaward and wasted shoreward
On shallows sheeted with flaming foam.

A grim, grey coast and a seaboard ghastly,
And shores trod seldom by feet of men —
Where the batter'd hull and the broken mast lie,
They have lain embedded these long years ten.
Love! when we wander'd here together,
Hand in hand through the sparkling weather,
From the heights and hollows of fern and heather,
God surely loved us a little then.

The influence of Swinburne (four years Gordon's junior) is unmistakable – but Swinburne, even when nodding, would not have rhymed 'ghastly' with 'mast lie'. However, though everything on this subject is conjecture, Emily would almost certainly have had Lawson on her shelves, and even at the grammar school his most famous lines – from *Ye Wearie Wayfarer* – would have been quoted, as they were to be quoted for a century more:

Question not, but live and labour
Till yon goal be won,
Helping every feeble neighbour,
Seeking help from none;
Life is mostly froth and bubble,
Two things stand like stone:
KINDNESS in another's trouble.
COURAGE in your own.

Barty Paterson is likely to have read Gordon, Harpur and Kendall during his schooldays or just after – Gordon had done much to revive an interest in the ballad, which was to become one of the Banjo's main interests. One of Kendall's most popular collections (in fact his last) was entitled *Bush Ballads and Galloping Rhymes* (1870), with such ballads as *The Sick Stockrider*, *The Rhyme of Joyous Garde* and *How we Beat the Favourite*. These certainly struck a vein of interest in Barty – the idea of telling a story in rhyme strongly appealed – and he may have found it expressed elsewhere in the work of contemporaries or near-contemporaries: Tennyson, for instance, and Browning. As for poetic form, an obvious influence seems to have been Swinburne, though it doesn't seem altogether likely that Emily would have pressed a volume of Swinburne's verse into young Barty's hands while he was still at school, for that poetry was still considered by many people to be erotic to the point of obscenity; even Browning was considered more than a little *risqué*, while Tennyson was safer.

Paterson's collected poems could safely be placed in the hands of any twelve-year old. He was not interested in the erotic side of life – at least not in the sense that he wanted to express it in verse. He wrote few love stories, fewer love poems – and this was perhaps as well, for those that we have are strongly tinted by Victorian sentimentality:

> *O, I love you, sweet, for your locks of brown*
> *   And the bluish on your cheek that lies —*
> *But I love you most for the kindly heart*
> *   That I see in your sweet blue eyes —*
> *For the eyes are signs of the soul within,*
> *   Of the heart that is leal and true,*
> *And my own sweetheart, I shall love you still*
> *   Just as long as your eyes are blue.*

Happily, his emotion, in poetry, went rather towards describing the Australian landscape and those who inhabited it – and, of course, horses; horses were always a passion, and perhaps his most deeply-felt verse celebrated or commemorated them, in for instance his deeply felt lament for those beasts which served in the Boer war and were then cast aside – *The Last Parade* (see pp.66-7), which no-one with a fellow-feeling for horses can surely read without sharing that emotion. (See also *DO They Know?*, p.225)

His first published verses, which came out in the *Bulletin* in 1885, when he was twenty-one, were political – a verse letter supposed to have been written by El Mahdi, who had led a rebellion against the Egyptian forces which had occupied the Sudan, asking why Australian troops should he sent against him. It was strongly felt, alluding to 'England's degenerate generals' and the Jews 'Squeezing the tax like blood from out the stone . . .' But as verse it was poor, imitative stuff:

> *"And wherefore have they come, this warlike band,*
> *That o'er the ocean many a weary day*
> *Have toss'd . . ."*

The editor of the *Bulletin* clearly realised, however, that whatever its value as verse, this was good combative stuff – Paterson's next published verses, entitled *The Bushfire*, dealt with British Prime Minister Gladstone's attempts to introduce an Irish Home Rule Bill. Comprehensible at the time, it is indifferent stuff today – but certainly the verse is tauter and Paterson's own tone of voice is beginning to emerge:

> *"Those coves as set your grass on fire*
> *There ain't no mortal doubt*
> *I've seen em ridin' here and there,*
> *And pokin' round about . . ."*

Indeed, Paterson found his own individual voice almost as soon as he began to publish – it is entirely recognisable in *The Mylora Elopement*, which came out in the *Bulletin* in December 1886, the opening lines of which, given the Swinburnean alliteration, is pure Banjo:

> By the winding Woolondilly where the weeping
>   willows weep,
> And the shepherd with his billy half awake and
>   half asleep
> Folds his fleecy flocks that linger homewards in
>   the setting sun,
> Lived my hero, Jim the Ringer, "cocky" on
>   Mylora run.

Horses, of course, share the action with the eloping lovers:

> The sound of a whip comes faint and far,
> A rattle of hoofs, and here they are,
> In all their tameless pride . . .

Ballads were not The Banjo's only form. Though by far the greatest number of his verses were either 'stories' or sketches of the Australian way of life, he also used verse not only to tell stories, but to underline and advance his political and social point of view, his idea of the way Australia was going. He is usually at the top of his form in his ballads, but he was by no means a negligible versifier in most of the forms he tried. Technically there are flaws which he saw and corrected in his later work, but as far as the emotion and general style are concerned, he was already fully formed when he started to publish. The vein of sentimentality which sometimes, rather disconcertingly, shows itself in his work, emerges early, as in *Over the Range* (1887), in which a child explains that when people die, 'They go to the country over the range', and describes her idea of the heaven to which her parents have gone; the poet concludes that

> . . . when we come to the final change
> We shall meet with our loved one gone before
> To the beautiful country over the range.

The racial pride which can occasionally go too far for the modern reader can also be seen in his earliest published work: in *Only a Jockey*, for instance – a poem about the death of a fourteen-year-old boy which the *Gazette* also published in 1887 – Paterson complains that 'Negroes and foreigners' and 'the outer barbarian' have a greater claim on the Australian public's sympathy than the 'poor jockey boy'; though at the same time it must be said that the real drive of the poem is a complaint at the lack of concern shown for the boy, and the question 'What did he get from our famed Christianity?'

His 'political' poems are now plagued by the problem of relevance; the Labour and Liberal politicians to whom they allude, and the political situations, are mostly long-forgotten; and the poems are not fierce enough to overcome this disadvantage. There are certainly one or two which are still amusing – his greeting, for instance, to Lord Northcote when the latter was appointed Governor-General in 1904:

> We read in the press that Lord Northcote is here
> To take up Lord Tennyson's mission.
> 'Tis pleasant to find they have sent us a Peer,
> And a man of exalted position.
> It's his business to see that the Radical horde
> From loyalty's path does not swerve us;
> But his tastes, and the task, don't seem quite in accord
> For they say that His Lordship is nervous.
>
> Does he think that wild animals walk in the street,
> Where the wary marsupial is hopping?
> Does he think that the snake and the platypus meet
> And "bail up" the folk who go shopping?
> And that boomerangs fly round the scared passer-by
> Who has come all this way to observe us,
> While the blackfellow launches a spear at his
> eye?
> No wonder His Lordship is nervous . . . [94]

See also, for a light-hearted look at the subject, *The Duties of an Aide-de-camp* (p.249).

Though he, like everyone else, had to put up with an alien Governor-General, The Banjo was not specially keen on native politicians who kow-towed to Britain. When George Richard Dibbs, the Premier of New South Wales, ceased to be a Republican on being offered a knighthood, he sent off a squib to the *Bulletin* – one of the bitterest he ever wrote:

> This G. R. Dibbs was a stalwart man
> Who was built on a most extensive plan,
> And a regular staunch Republican.
>
> But he fell in the hands of the Tory crew
> Who said, "It's a shame that a man like you
> Should teach Australia this nasty view.
>
> "From her mother's side she should ne'er be gone
> And she ought to be glad to be smiled upon,
> And proud to be known as our hanger-on."
>
> And G. R. Dibbs, he went off his peg
> At the swells who came for his smiles to beg
> And the Prince of Wales — who was pulling his leg . . .
>
> So he strutted along with the titled band
> And he sold the pride of his native land
> For a bow and a smile and a shake of the hand.
>
> And the Tory drummers they sit and call:
> "Send over your leaders great and small
> For the price is low, and we'll buy them all
>
> "With a tinsel title, a tawdry star
> Of a lower grade than our titles are,
> And a puff at a Prince's big cigar."
>
> And the Tories laugh till they crack their ribs
> When they think how they purchased G. R. Dibbs.[95]

He laid about him, too, when the banks failed in 1893, and a Bill was passed in Parliament declaring the banks' IOUs legal tender, and transferring their assets to new, 'reconstructed' banks.

> *So, the bank has bust its boiler! And in six or*
> *seven year*
> *It will pay me all my money back — of course!*
> *But the horse will perish waiting while the*
> *grass is germinating,*
> *And I reckon I'll be something like the horse.*
>
> *There's the ploughing to be finished and the*
> *ploughmen want their pay*
> *And I'd like to wire the fence and sink a tank;*
> *But I own I'm fairly beat how I'm going to*
> *make ends meet*
> *With my money in a reconstructed bank . . .*
>
> *And their profits from the business have been*
> *twenty-five per cent,*
> *Which, I reckon, is a pretty tidy whack,*
> *And I think it's only proper, now the*
> *thing has come a cropper,*
> *That they ought to pay a little of it back...*[96]

Very occasionally The Banjo used verse a touch too obviously to express his own prejudices – his pessimistic view of the 'yellow peril' for instance – as when he read that a man called McGuinness and his wife were leaving the country because he could not get work:

> *But perhaps — later on — when the Chow and*
> *the Jap*
> *Begin to drift down from the tropics,*
> *When a big yellow stain spreading over the map*
> *Provides some disquieting topics,*
>
> *Oh, it's then when they're wanting a man that*
> *will stand*

> *In the trench where his own kith and kin is,*
> *With a frown on his face and a gun in his hand—*
> *Then there might be a job for McGuinness!* [97]

But the Banjo's reputation really rests on his 'bush ballads'. He clearly recognised early on the power of poetry as an instrument for story-telling. There is a view that this is how poetry began: as story-telling in a form which could be recited or sung, a way of recording and remembering tales of one sort and another; in the beginning poetry indeed was probably completely oral, originating before the invention of writing, and the earliest poem we have, the *Epic of Gilgamesh* (a story if ever there was one) though written down in the fourth millennium BC on clay tablets, undoubtedly originated earlier as recitation, verse remembered and passed down from one generation to the next.

The Banjo's best ballads are in a strict sense not ballads at all – *Old Pardon, the Son of Reprieve*, for instance, probably his earliest, and his best-known, *The Man from Snowy River*. He was not preoccupied with form – though he clearly had some knowledge of prosody – for instance sniffing contemptuously at some areas of it:

> *Of all the sickly forms of verse,*
>   *Commend me to the triolet.*
> *It makes bad writers somewhat worse:*
> *Of all the sickly forms of verse*
> *That fall beneath a reader's curse.*
>   *It is the feeblest jingle yet.*
> *Of all the sickly forms of verse*
>   *Commend me to the triolet.*

But we need not concern ourselves at his ballads not being written in the traditional ballad metres – in quatrains (the traditional four-line verses) and alternate iambic tetrameters and trimeters (*Brumby's Run*, see p.198, is one of very few written in that form). The point is that he used his ballads to record and celebrate a way of life which he saw as basically and individually Australian, and that they came to him, in Keats' celebrated phrase, 'as easily as the leaves to the tree'.

Paterson joined and became one of the leading personalities of a small but influential band of 'bush balladeers' some of whose names are familiar, others who remain unknown – those men who, like the unknown composers of traditional folk-songs, snatched melodies and words from the air and sent them out to be sung and recited by thousands of others who never knew from whence they came. They sprung from everyday life and frequently from its harshness; they spoke of the lives of miners and farmers, drovers and shearers, of their struggle to find work and the toughness of working conditions when they found it, of squatters and outlaws, fights with greedy landowners, and of their wives and lovers.

Many of the earliest bush ballads were rooted, in a sense, in Europe – at least the form they took came to Australia with the earliest settlers who when they were growing up would have learned

> Come, gentlemen all, and listen a while:
> A story I'll to you unfold —
> How Robin Hood servèd the Bishop
> When he robb'd him of his gold.

> In Scarlet town, where I was born
> There was a fair maid dwellin'
> Made every youth cry Well-a-way!
> Her name was Barbara Allen.

> The wind doth blow today, my love,
> And a few small drops of rain;
> I never had but one true-love;
> In cold grave she was lain.

In the hands of the early Australian balladeers the history of Robin Hood became the story of an outlaw, a renegade trooper or an out-and-outer from Lobbs' Hole, while the death of a noble knight became the simple request of a dying stockman:

> *Wrap me up with my stockwhip and blanket,*
> *And bury me deep down below,*
> *Where the dingoes and crows can't molest me,*
> *In the shade where the coolibahs grow.*

As John Stratton has pointed out[98], the ballad as a form of popular entertainment had almost died out in Great Britain by the 1860s; the music hall had taken over, and music-hall songs (*Champagne Charlie*, *Any Old Iron* and *Boiled Beef and Carrots*, to name a few) had almost completely replaced the old ballads which used to be sung in pubs or around the piano at home. But in Australia there was no such phenomenon – not for some years, and then certainly not outside the largest towns. So the ballad as form continued to thrive and was modified by influences from settlers from all over Europe, and indeed from America and Asia.

Many of the early Australian bush ballads were sung – *The Dying Stockman* is a case in point; others, including The Banjo's – apart (of course) from *Waltzing Matilda* – were not; but this was not unusual in the history of European ballads, many of which originated as printed broadsheets sold for a penny or two, to be learned or simply (like the early astrological almanacs) stuck on a wall for decoration. The newspapers in which Paterson's verses appeared were the modern equivalent and also published the work of his contemporaries. We cannot know how many of their ballads were actually learned, read or recited at informal gatherings and entertainments, but the speed with which *Clancy of the Overflow* or *The Man from Snowy River* became current suggests that this probably happened a great deal.

That he became the nearest thing Australia has to a popular national poet – and though this, as The Banjo freely admitted, bore little relation to anyone's definition of a 'great' poet writing 'great' poetry – is not surprising when one considers the subjects about which he wrote, the keenness of his observation and the emotion and liveliness of his work. In the most dissimilar possible of genres, he is to Australia what John Betjeman is to England – to read both is immediately to be carried into the landscape they loved, to see the people that most intrigued and captivated then, and to feel the passion each had for his own country and its ways.

A Selection of Banjo Paterson's Poetry

Waltzing Matilda

Oh! there once was a swagman camped in a Billabong,
Under the shade of a Coolabah tree;
And he sang as he looked at his old billy boiling,
'Who'll come a-waltzing Matilda with me?'

Who'll come a-waltzing Matilda, my darling?
Who'll come a-waltzing Matilda with me?
Waltzing Matilda and leading a water-bag -
Who'll come a-waltzing Matilda with me?

Down came a jumbuck to drink at the water-hole,
Up jumped the swagman and grabbed him with glee;
And he sang as he stowed him away in his tucker-bag,
'You'll come a-waltzing Matilda with me.'

Down came the Squatter a-riding his thoroughbred;
Down came Policemen - one, two and three.
'Whose is the jumbuck you've got in the tucker-bag?
You'll come a-waltzing Matilda with me!'

But the swagman he up and he jumped in the water-hole,
Drowning himself by the Coolabah tree;
And his ghost may be heard as it sings in the Billabong
'Who'll come a-waltzing Matilda with me?'

Clancy of the Overflow

I had written him a letter which I had, for want of better
Knowledge, sent to where I met him down the Lachlan, years ago,
He was shearing when I knew him, so I sent the letter to him,
Just *on spec*, addressed as follows, 'Clancy, of The Overflow'

And an answer came directed in a writing unexpected,
(And I think the same was written with a thumb-nail dipped in tar)
Twas his shearing mate who wrote it, and *verbatim* I will quote it:
'Clancy's gone to Queensland droving, and we don't know
     where he are.'

* * *

In my wild erratic fancy visions come to me of Clancy
Gone a-droving 'down the Cooper' where the Western
     drovers go;
As the stock are slowly stringing, Clancy rides behind them singing,
For the drover's life has pleasures that the townsfolk never know.

And the bush hath friends to meet him, and their kindly
     voices greet him
In the murmur of the breezes and the river on its bars,
And he sees the vision splendid of the sunlit plains extended,
And at night the wond'rous glory of the everlasting stars.

* * *

I am sitting in my dingy little office, where a stingy
Ray of sunlight struggles feebly down between the houses tall,
And the foetid air and gritty of the dusty, dirty city
Through the open window floating, spreads its foulness over all

And in place of lowing cattle, I can hear the fiendish rattle
Of the tramways and the buses making hurry down the street,
And the language uninviting of the gutter children fighting,
Comes fitfully and faintly through the ceaseless tramp of feet.

And the hurrying people daunt me, and their pallid faces
   haunt me
As they shoulder one another in their rush and nervous haste,
With their eager eyes and greedy, and their stunted forms
   and weedy,
For townsfolk have no time to grow, they have no time to waste.

And I somehow rather fancy that I'd like to change with Clancy,
Like to take a turn at droving where the seasons come and go,
While he faced the round eternal of the cash-book and the journal --
But I doubt he'd suit the office, Clancy, of The Overflow.

Old Pardon, the Son of Reprieve

You never heard tell of the story?
Well, now, I can hardly believe!
Never heard of the honour and glory
Of Pardon, the son of Reprieve?
But maybe you're only a Johnnie
And don't know a horse from a hoe?
Well, well, don't get angry, my sonny,
But, really, a young un should know.

They bred him out back on the 'Never',
His mother was Mameluke breed.
To the front - and then stay there - was ever
The root of the Mameluke creed.
He seemed to inherit their wiry
Strong frames - and their pluck to receive -
As hard as a flint and as fiery
Was Pardon, the son of Reprieve.

We ran him at many a meeting
At crossing and gully and town,
And nothing could give him a beating -
At least when our money was down.
For weight wouldn't stop him, nor distance,
Nor odds, though the others were fast;
He'd race with a dogged persistence,
And wear them all down at the last.

At the Turon the Yattendon filly
Led by lengths at the mile-and-a-half,
And we all began to look silly,
While her crowd were starting to laugh;
But the old horse came faster and faster,
His pluck told its tale, and his strength,
He gained on her, caught her, and passed her,
And won it, hands down, by a length.

And then we swooped down on Menindie
To run for the President's Cup;
Oh! that's a sweet township - a shindy
To them is board, lodging, and sup.
Eye-openers they are, and their system
Is never to suffer defeat;
It's 'win, tie, or wrangle' - to best 'em
You must lose 'em, or else it's 'dead heat'.

We strolled down the township and found 'em
At drinking and gaming and play;
If sorrows they had, why they drowned 'em,
And betting was soon under way.
Their horses were good uns and fit uns,
There was plenty of cash in the town;
They backed their own horses like Britons,
And, Lord! how *we* rattled it down!

With gladness we thought of the morrow,
We counted our wages with glee,
A simile homely to borrow -
'There was plenty of milk in our tea.'
You see we were green; and we never
Had even a thought of foul play,
Though we well might have known that the clever
Division would 'put us away'.

Experience docet, they tell us,
At least so I've frequently heard;
But, 'dosing' or 'stuffing', those fellows
Were up to each move on the board:
They got to his stall - it is sinful
To think what such villains will do -
And they gave him a regular skinful
Of barley - green barley - to chew.

He munched it all night, and we found him
Next morning as full as a hog -
The girths wouldn't nearly meet round him;
He looked like an overfed frog.
We saw we were done like a dinner -
The odds were a thousand to one
Against Pardon turning up winner,
'Twas cruel to ask him to run.

We got to the course with our troubles,
A crestfallen couple were we;
And we heard the 'books' calling the doubles -
A roar like the surf of the sea.
And over the tumult and louder
Rang 'Any price Pardon, I lay!'
Says Jimmy, 'The children of Judah
Are out on the warpath today.'

Three miles in three heats: - Ah, my sonny,
The horses in those days were stout,
They had to run well to win money;
I don't see such horses about.
Your six-furlong vermin that scamper
Half-a-mile with their feather-weight up,
They wouldn't earn much of their damper
In a race like the President's Cup.

The first heat was soon set a-going;
The Dancer went off to the front;
The Don on his quarters was showing,
With Pardon right out of the hunt.
He rolled and he weltered and wallowed -
You'd kick your hat faster, I'll bet;
They finished all bunched, and he followed
All lathered and dripping with sweat.

But troubles came thicker upon us,
For while we were rubbing him dry
The stewards came over to warn us:
'We hear you are running a bye!
If Pardon don't spiel like tarnation
And win the next heat - if he can -
He'll earn a disqualification;
Just think over *that* now, my man!'

Our money all gone and our credit,
Our horse couldn't gallop a yard;
And then people thought that *we* did it
It really was terribly hard.
We were objects of mirth and derision
To folks in the lawn and the stand,
And the yells of the clever division
Of 'Any price Pardon!' were grand.

We still had a chance for the money,
Two heats remained to be run:
If both fell to us - why, my sonny,
The clever division were done.
And Pardon was better, we reckoned,
His sickness was passing away,
So we went to the post for the second
And principal heat of the day.

They're off and away with a rattle,
Like dogs from the leashes let slip,
And right at the back of the battle
He followed them under the whip.
They gained ten good lengths on him quickly
He dropped right away from the pack;
I tell you it made me feel sickly
To see the blue jacket fall back.

Our very last hope had departed -
We thought the old fellow was done,
When all of a sudden he started
To go like a shot from a gun.
His chances seemed slight to embolden
Our hearts; but, with teeth firmly set,
We thought, 'Now or never! The old un
May reckon with some of 'em yet.'

Then loud rose the war-cry for Pardon;
He swept like the wind down the dip,
And over the rise by the garden
The jockey was done with the whip.
The field was at sixes and sevens -
The pace at the first had been fast -
And hope seemed to drop from the heavens,
For Pardon was coming at last.

And how he did come! It was splendid;
He gained on them yards every bound,
Stretching out like a greyhound extended,
His girth laid right down on the ground.
A shimmer of silk in the cedars
As into the running they wheeled,
And out flashed the whips on the leaders,
For Pardon had collared the field.

Then right through the ruck he was sailing -
I knew that the battle was won -
The son of Haphazard was failing,
The Yattendon filly was done;
He cut down The Don and The Dancer,
He raced clean away from the mare -
He's in front! Catch him now if you can, sir!
And up went my hat in the air!

Then loud from the lawn and the garden
Rose offers of 'Ten to one *on!*
'Who'll bet on the field? I back Pardon!'
No use; all the money was gone.
He came for the third heat light-hearted,
A-jumping and dancing about;
The others were done ere they started
Crestfallen, and tired, and worn out.

He won it, and ran it much faster
Than even the first, I believe;
Oh, he was the daddy, the master,
Was Pardon, the son of Reprieve.
He showed 'em the method of travel -
The boy sat still as a stone -
They never could see him for gravel;
He came in hard-held, and alone.

* * *

But he's old - and his eyes are grown hollow
Like me, with my thatch of the snow;
When he dies, then I hope I may follow,
And go where the racehorses go.
I don't want no harping nor singing -
Such things with my style don't agree;
Where the hoofs of the horses are ringing
There's music sufficient for me.

And surely the thoroughbred horses
Will rise up again and begin
Fresh faces on far-away courses,
And p'raps they might let me slip in.
It would look rather well the race-card on
'Mongst Cherubs and Seraphs and things,
'Angel Harrison's black gelding Pardon,
Blue halo, white body and wings.'

And if they have racing hereafter,
(And who is to say they will not?)
When the cheers and the shouting and laughter
Proclaim that the battle grows hot;
As they come down the racecourse a-steering,
He'll rush to the front, I believe;
And you'll hear the great multitude cheering
For Pardon, the son of Reprieve.

In the Droving Days

'Only a pound,' said the auctioneer,
'Only a pound; and I'm standing here
Selling this animal, gain or loss -
Only a pound for the drover's horse?
One of the sort that was ne'er afraid,
One of the boys of the Old Brigade;
Thoroughly honest and game, I'll swear,
Only a little the worse for wear;
Plenty as bad to be seen in town,
Give me a bid and I'll knock him down;
Sold as he stands, and without recourse,
Give me a bid for the drover's horse.'

Loitering there in an aimless way
Somehow I noticed the poor old grey,
Weary and battered and screwed, of course;
Yet when I noticed the old grey horse,
The rough bush saddle, and single rein
Of the bridle laid on his tangled mane,
Straightway the crowd and the auctioneer
Seemed on a sudden to disappear,
Melted away in a kind of haze -
For my heart went back to the droving days.

Back to the road, and I crossed again
Over the miles of the saltbush plain -
The shining plain that is said to be
The dried-up bed of an inland sea.
Where the air so dry and so clear and bright
Refracts the sun with a wondrous light,
And out in the dim horizon makes
The deep blue gleam of the phantom lakes.

At dawn of day we could feel the breeze
That stirred the boughs of the sleeping trees,
And brought a breath of the fragrance rare
That comes and goes in that scented air;
For the trees and grass and the shrubs contain
A dry sweet scent on the saltbush plain.
for those that love it and understand
The saltbush plain is a wonderland,
A wondrous country, where Nature's ways
Were revealed to me in the droving days.

We saw the fleet wild horses pass,
And kangaroos through the Mitchell grass;
The emu ran with her frightened brood
All unmolested and unpursued.
But there rose a shout and a wild hubbub
When the dingo raced for his native scrub,
And he paid right dear for his stolen meals
With the drovers' dogs at his wretched heels.
For we ran him down at a rattling pace,
While the pack-horse joined in the stirring chase.
And a wild halloo at the kill we'd raise -
We were light of heart in the droving days.

'Twas a drover's horse, and my hand again
Made a move to close on a fancied rein.
For I felt a swing and the easy stride
Of the grand old horse that I used to ride.
In drought or plenty, in good or ill,
The same old steed was my comrade still;
The old grey horse with his honest ways
Was a mate to me in the droving days.

When we kept our watch in the cold and damp,
If the cattle broke from the sleeping camp,
Over the flats and across the plain,
With my head bent down on his waving mane,

Through the boughs above and the stumps below,
On the darkest night I could let him go
At a racing speed; he would choose his course,
And my life was safe with the old grey horse.
But man and horse had a favourite job,
When an outlaw broke from the station mob;
With a right good will was the stockwhip plied,
As the old horse raced at the straggler's side,
And the greenhide whip such a weal would raise -
We could use the whip in the droving days.

* * *

'Only a pound!' and was this the end -
Only a pound for the drover's friend.
The drover's friend that has seen his day,
And now was worthless and cast away
With a broken knee and a broken heart
To be flogged and starved in a hawker's cart.
Well, I made a bid for a sense of shame
And the memories of the good old game.

'Thank you? Guinea! and cheap at that!
Against you there in the curly hat!
Only a guinea, and one more chance,
Down he goes if there's no advance,
Third, and last time, one! two! three!'
And the old grey horse was knocked down to me.
And now he's wandering, fat and sleek,
On the lucerne flats by the Homestead Creek;
I dare not ride him for fear he'll fall,
But he does a journey to beat them all,
For though he scarcely a trot can raise,
He can take me back to the droving days.

The Man from Snowy River

There was movement at the station, for the word had passed around
That the colt from Old Regret had got away,
And had joined the wild bush horses - he was worth a
    thousand pound
So all the cracks had gathered to the fray.
All the tried and noted riders from the stations near and far
Had mustered at the homestead overnight,
For the bushmen love hard riding where the wild bush horses are,
And the stock-horse snuffs the battle with delight.

There was Harrison, who made his pile when Pardon won the cup,
The old man with his hair as white as snow;
But few could ride beside him when his blood was fairly up -
He would go wherever horse and man could go.
And Clancy of the Overflow came down to lend a hand,
No better horseman ever held the reins;
For never horse could throw him while the saddle-girths
    would stand,
He learnt to ride while droving on the plains.

And one was there, a stripling on a small and weedy beast,
He was something like a racehorse undersized,
With a touch of Timor pony - three parts thoroughbred at least -
And such as are by mountain horsemen prized.
He was hard and tough and wiry - just the sort that won't say die -
There was courage in his quick impatient tread;
And he bore the badge of gameness in his bright and fiery eye,
And the proud and lofty carriage of his head.

But still so slight and weedy, one would doubt his power to stay,
And the old man said, 'That horse will never do
For a long and tiring gallop - lad, you'd better stop away,
Those hills are far too rough for such as you.'
So he waited sad and wistful - only Clancy stood his friend -
I think we ought to let him come,' he said;

'I warrant he'll be with us when he's wanted at the end,
For both his horse and he are mountain bred.'

'He hails from Snowy River, up by Kosciusko's side,
Where the hills are twice as steep and twice as rough,
Where a horse's hoofs strike firelight from the flint stones
    every stride,
The man that holds his own is good enough.
And the Snowy River riders on the mountains make their home,
Where the river runs those giant hills between;
I have seen full many horsemen since I first commenced to roam,
But nowhere yet such horsemen have I seen.'

So he went - they found the horses by the big mimosa clump --
They raced away towards the mountain's brow,
And the old man gave his orders, 'Boys, go at them from the jump,
No use to try for fancy riding now.
And, Clancy, you must wheel them, try and wheel them to
    the right.
Ride boldly, lad, and never fear the spills,
For never yet was rider that could keep the mob in sight,
If once they gain the shelter of those hills.'

So Clancy rode to wheel them - he was racing on the wing
Where the best and boldest riders take their place,
And he raced his stock-horse past them, and he made the
    ranges ring
With the stockwhip, as he met them face to face.
Then they halted for a moment, while he swung the dreaded
lash,
But they saw their well-loved mountain full in view,
And they charged beneath the stockwhip with a sharp and
    sudden dash,
And off into the mountain scrub they flew.

Then fast the horsemen followed, where the gorges deep and black
Resounded to the thunder of their tread,
And the stockwhips woke the echoes, and they fiercely
    answered back
From cliffs and crags that beetled overhead.
And upward, ever upward, the wild horses held their way,
Where mountain ash and kurrajong grew wide;
And the old man muttered fiercely, 'We may bid the mob
    good day,
No man can hold them down the other side.'

When they reached the mountain's summit, even Clancy took
    a pull,
It well might make the boldest hold their breath,
The wild hop scrub grew thickly, and the hidden ground was full
Of wombat holes, and any slip was death.
But the man from Snowy River let the pony have his head,
And he swung his stockwhip round and gave a cheer,
And he raced him down the mountain like a torrent down its bed,
While the others stood and watched in very fear.

He sent the flint stones flying, but the pony kept his feet,
He cleared the fallen timber in his stride,
And the man from Snowy River never shifted in his seat -
It was grand to see that mountain horseman ride.
Through the stringy barks and saplings, on the rough and
    broken ground,
Down the hillside at a racing pace he went;
And he never drew the bridle till he landed safe and sound,
At the bottom of that terrible descent.

He was right among the horses as they climbed the further hill,
And the watchers on the mountain standing mute,
Saw him ply the stockwhip fiercely, he was right among them still,
As he raced across the clearing in pursuit.
Then they lost him for a moment, where two mountain gullies met
In the ranges, but a final glimpse reveals

On a dim and distant hillside the wild horses racing yet,
With the man from Snowy River at their heels..

And he ran them single-handed till their sides were white with foam.
He followed like a bloodhound on their track,
Till they halted cowed and beaten, then he turned their heads
   for home,
And alone and unassisted brought them back..
But his hardy mountain pony he could scarcely raise a trot,
He was blood from hip to shoulder from the spur;
But his pluck was still undaunted, and his courage fiery hot,
For never yet was mountain horse a cur.

And down by Kosciusko, where the pine-clad ridges raise
Their torn and rugged battlements on high,
Where the air is clear as crystal, and the white stars fairly blaze
At midnight in the cold and frosty sky,
And where around the Overflow the reedbeds sweep and sway
To the breezes, and the rolling plains are wide,
The man from Snowy River is a household word to-day,
And the stockmen tell the story of his ride.

Lost

'He ought to be home,' said the old man, 'without there's
   something amiss.
He only went to the Two-mile - he ought to be back by this.
He *would* ride the Reckless filly, he *would* have his wilful way;
And, here, he's not back at sundown - and what will his
   mother say?'

'He was always his mother's idol, since ever his father died;
And there isn't a horse on the station that he isn't game to ride.
But that Reckless mare is vicious, and if once she gets away
He hasn't got strength to hold her - and what will his mother say?'

The old man walked to the sliprail, and peered up the dark'ning
   track,
And looked and longed for the rider that would never more
   come back;
And the mother came and clutched him, with sudden,
   spasmodic fright:
'What has become of my Willie? Why isn't he home tonight?'

Away in the gloomy ranges, at the foot of an ironbark,
The bonnie, winsome laddie was lying stiff and stark;
For the Reckless mare had smashed him against a leaning limb,
And his comely face was battered, and his merry eyes were dim.

And the thoroughbred chestnut filly, the saddle beneath her flanks,
Was away like fire through the ranges to join the wild mob's ranks;
And a broken-hearted woman and an old man worn and grey
Were searching all night in the ranges till the sunrise brought
the day.

And the mother kept feebly calling, with a hope that would not die,
'Willie! where are you, Willie?' But how can the dead reply;
And hope died out with the daylight, and the darkness
   brought despair,
God pity the stricken mother, and answer the widow's prayer!
Though far and wide they sought him, they found not where he fell;
For the ranges held him precious, and guarded their treasure well.
The wattle blooms above him, and the bluebells blow close by,
And the brown bees buzz the secret, and the wild birds sing reply.

But the mother pined and faded, and cried, and took no rest,
And rode each day to the ranges on her hopeless, weary quest.
Seeking her loved one ever, she faded and pined away,
But with strength of her great affection she still sought every
day.

'I know that sooner or later I shall find my boy,' she said.
But she came not home one evening, and they found her lying dead.
And stamped on the poor pale features, as the spirit
   homeward pass'd,
Was an angel smile of gladness - she had found the boy at last.

The Geebung Polo Club

It was somewhere up the country, in a land of rock and scrub,
That they formed an institution called the Geebung Polo Club.
There were long and wiry natives from the rugged mountain
side,
And the horse was never saddled that the Geebungs couldn't ride;
But their style of playing polo was irregular and rash --
They had mighty little science, but a mighty lot of dash:
And they played on mountain ponies that were muscular and strong,
Though their coats were quite unpolished, and their manes
and tails were long.
And they used to train those ponies wheeling cattle in the scrub;
They were demons, were the members of the Geebung Polo Club.

It was somewhere down the country, in a city's smoke and steam,
That a polo club existed, called the 'Cuff and Collar Team'.
As a social institution 'twas a marvellous success,
For the members were distinguished by exclusiveness and dress.
They had natty little ponies that were nice, and smooth, and sleek,
For their cultivated owners only rode 'em once a week.
So they started up the country in pursuit of sport and fame,
For they meant to show the Geebungs how they ought to play
  the game;
And they took their valets with them - just to give their boots a rub
Ere they started operations on the Geebung Polo Club.

Now my readers can imagine how the contest ebbed and flowed,
When the Geebung boys got going it was time to clear the road;
And the game was so terrific that ere half the time was gone
A spectator's leg was broken - just from merely looking on.
For they waddied one another till the plain was strewn with dead,
While the score was kept so even that they neither got ahead.

And the Cuff and Collar Captain, when he tumbled off to die
Was the last surviving player - so the game was called a tie.

Then the Captain of the Geebungs raised him slowly from the
ground,
Though his wounds were mostly mortal, yet he fiercely gazed around;
There was no one to oppose him - all the rest were in a trance,
So he scrambled on his pony for his last expiring chance,
For he meant to make an effort to get victory to his side;
So he struck at goal - and missed it - then he tumbled off and died.

* * *

By the old Campaspe River, where the breezes shake the grass,
There's a row of little gravestones that the stockmen never pass,
For they bear a rude inscription saying, 'Stranger, drop a tear,
For the Cuff and Collar players and the Geebung boys lie here.'
And on misty moonlit evenings, while the dingoes howl around,
You can see their shadows flitting down that phantom polo ground;
You can hear the loud collisions as the flying players meet,
And the rattle of the mallets, and the rush of ponies' feet,
Till the terrified spectator rides like blazes to the pub -
He's been haunted by the spectres of the Geebung Polo Club.

The Amateur Rider

Him goin' to ride for us! *Him* - with the pants and the
   eyeglass and all.
Amateur! don't he just look it - it's twenty to one on a fall.
Boss must be gone off his head to be sending out steeplechase crack
Out over fences like these with an object like that on his back.

Ride! Don't tell *me* he can ride. With his pants just as loose
   as balloons,
How can he sit on a horse? and his spurs like a pair of harpoons;
Ought to be under the Dog Act, he ought, and be kept off
   the course.
Fall! why, he'd fall off a cart, let alone off a steeplechase horse.

* * *

Yessir! the 'orse is all ready - I wish you'd have rode him before;
Nothing like knowing your 'orse, sir, and this chap's a terror to bore;
Battleaxe always could pull, and he rushes his fences like fun -
Stands off his jump twenty feet, and then springs like a shot
from a gun.

Oh, he can jump 'em all right, sir, you make no mistake, 'e's a toff -
Clouts 'em in earnest, too, sometimes; you mind that he don't
   clout you off -
Don't seem to mind how he hits 'em, his shins is as hard as a nail,
Sometimes you'll see the fence shake and the splinters fly up
from the rail.

All you can do is to hold him and just let him jump as he likes,
Give him his head at the fences, and hang on like death if he strikes;
Don't let him run himself out - you can lie third or fourth in
   the race -
Until you clear the stone wall, and from that you can put on
the pace.

Fell at that wall once, he did, and it gave him a regular spread,
Ever since that time he flies it - he'll stop if you pull at his head,
Just let him race - you can trust him - he'll take first-class care
   he don't fall,
And I think that's the lot - but remember, he must have his
head at the wall.

* * *

Well, he's down safe as far as the start, and he seems to sit on
   pretty neat,
Only his baggified breeches would ruinate anyone's seat -
They're away - here they come - the first fence, and he's head
   over heels for a crown!
Good for the new chum! he's over, and two of the others are down!

Now for the treble, my hearty - By Jove, he can ride, after all;
Whoop, that's your sort - let him fly them! He hasn't much
   fear of a fall.
Who in the world would have thought it? And aren't they just
   going a pace?
Little Recruit in the lead there will make it a stoutly-run race.

Lord! but they're racing in earnest - and down goes Recruit on
   his head,
Rolling clean over his boy - it's a miracle if he ain't dead.
Battleaxe, Battleaxe, yet! By the Lord, he's got most of 'em beat -
Ho! did you see how he struck, and the swell never moved in
his seat?

Second time round, and, by Jingo! he's holding his lead of 'em well;
Hark to him clouting the timber! It don't seem to trouble the swell.
Now for the wall - let him rush it. A thirty-foot leap, I declare -
Never a shift in his seat, and he's racing for home like a hare.

What's that that's chasing him - Rataplan - regular demon to stay!
Sit down and ride for your life now! Oh, good, that's the style
- come away!

Rataplan's certain to beat you, unless you can give him the slip,
Sit down and rub in the whalebone - now give him the spurs
and the whip!

Battleaxe, Battleaxe, yet - and it's Battleaxe wins for a crown;
Look at him rushing the fences, he wants to bring t'other
  chap down.
Rataplan never will catch him if only he keeps on his pins;
Now! the last fence, and he's over it! Battleaxe, Battleaxe wins!

* * *

Well, sir, you rode him just perfect - I knew from the fust you
  could ride.
Some of the chaps said you couldn't, an' I says just like this a'
  one side:
Mark me, I says, that's a tradesman - the saddle is where he
  was bred.
Weight! you're all right, sir, and thank you; and tham was the
words that I said.

Last Week

Oh, the new-chum went to the backblock run,
But he should have gone there last week.
He tramped ten miles with a loaded gun,
But of turkey or duck saw never a one,
For he should have been there last week,
They said,
There were flocks of 'em there last week.

He wended his way to a waterfall,
And he should have gone there last week.
He carried a camera, legs and all,
But the day was hot and the stream was small,
For he should have gone there last week,
They said,
They drowned a man there last week.

He went for a drive, and he made a start,
Which should have been made last week,
For the old horse died of a broken heart;
So he footed it home and he dragged the cart --
But the horse was all right last week,
They said,
He trotted a match last week.

So he asked all the bushies who came from afar
To visit the town last week
If they'd dine with him, and they said 'Hurrah!'
But there wasn't a drop in the whisky jar --
You should have been here last week,
He said,
I drank it all up last week!

Johnson's Antidote

Down along the Snakebite River where the overlanders camp,
Where the serpents are in millions, all of the most deadly stamp;
Where the station-cook in terror, nearly every time he bakes,
Mixes up among the doughboys half a dozen poison-snakes;
Where the wily free-selector walks in armour-plated pants,
And defies the stings of scorpions, and the bites of bull-dog ants:
Where the adder and the viper tear each other by the throat -
There it was that William Johnson sought his snake-bite antidote.

Johnson was a free-selector, and his brain went rather queer,
For the constant sight of serpents filled him with a deadly fear;
So he tramped his free selection, morning, afternoon, and night,
Seeking for some great specific that would cure the serpent's bite
Till King Billy, of the Mooki, chieftain of the flour-bag head,
Told him, 'Spos'n snake bite pfeller, pfeller mostly drop down dead;
Spos'n snake bite old goanna, then you watch a while you see
Old goanna cure himself with eating little pfeller tree.'
'That's the cure,' said William Johnson, 'point me out this plant sublime,'
But King Billy, feeling lazy, said he'd go another time.
Thus it came to pass that Johnson, having got the tale by rote,
Followed every stray goanna seeking for the antidote.

* * *

Loafing once beside the river, while he thought his heart
  would break,
There he saw a big goanna fight with a tiger-snake.
In and out they rolled and wriggled, bit each other, heart and soul,
Till the valiant old goanna swallowed his opponent whole.
Breathless, Johnson sat and watched him, saw him struggle up
  the bank,
Saw him nibbling at the branches of some bushes, green and rank;
Saw him, happy and contented, lick his lips, as off he crept,
While the bulging of his stomach showed where his opponent slept.

Then a cheer of exultation burst aloud from Johnson's throat;
'Luck at last,' said he, 'I've struck it! 'tis the famous antidote.

'Here it is, the Grand Elixir, greatest blessing ever known -
Twenty thousand men in India die each year of snakes alone;
Think of all the foreign nations, negro, chow, and blackamoor,
Saved from sudden expiration by my wondrous snakebite cure.
It will bring me fame and fortune! In the happy days to be
Men of every clime and nation will be round to gaze on me -
Scientific men in thousands, men of mark and men of note,
Rushing down the Mooki River, after Johnson's antidote.
It will cure *delirium tremens* when the patient's eyeballs stare
At imaginary spiders, snakes which really are not there.
When he thinks he sees them wriggle, when he thinks he sees
    them bloat,
It will cure him just to think of Johnson's Snakebite Antidote.'

Then he rushed to the museum, found a scientific man -
'Trot me out a deadly serpent, just the deadliest you can;
I intend to let him bite me, all the risk I will endure
Just to prove the sterling value of my wondrous snakebite cure.
Even though an adder bit me, back to life again I'd float;
Snakes are out of date, I tell you, since I've found the antidote.'
Said the scientific person, 'If you really want to die,
Go ahead - but, if you're doubtful, let your sheep-dog have a try.
Get a pair of dogs and try it, let the snake give both a nip;
Give your dog the snakebite mixture, let the other fellow rip;
If he dies and your's survives him then it proves the thing is good.
Will you fetch your dog and try it?' Johnson rather thought
    he would.
So he went and fetched his canine, hauled him forward by the throat.
'Stump, old man,' says he, 'we'll show them we've the genwine
    antidote.'

Both the dogs were duly loaded with the poison gland's contents;
Johnson gave his dog the mixture, then sat down to wait events.
'Mark,' he said, 'in twenty minutes Stump'll be a-rushing round,

While the other wretched creature lies a corpse upon the ground.'
But, alas for William Johnson! ere they's watched a half-hour's spell
Stumpy was as dead as mutton, t'other dog was live and well.
And the scientific person hurried off with utmost speed,
Tested Johnson's drug and found it was deadly poison-weed;
Half a tumbler killed an emu, half a spoonful killed a goat -
All the snakes on earth were harmless to that awful antidote.

Down along the Mooki River, on the overlanders' camp,
Where the serpents are in millions, all of the most deadly stamp,
Wanders, daily, William Johnson, down among those
    poisonous hordes,
Shooting every stray goanna, calls them 'black and yaller frauds'.
And King Billy, of the Mooki, cadging for the cast-off coat,
Somehow seems to dodge the subject of the snakebite antidote.

Father Riley's Horse

'Twas the horse thief, Andy Regan, that was hunted like a dog
By the troopers of the upper Murray side,
They had searched in every gully - they had looked in every log,
But never sight or track of him they spied,
Till the priest at Kiley's Crossing heard a knocking very late
And a whisper 'Father Riley - come across!'
So his Rev'rence in pyjamas trotted softly to the gate
And admitted Andy Regan - and a horse!

'Now, it's listen, Father Riley, to the words I've got to say,
For it's close upon my death I am tonight.
With the troopers hard behind me I've been hiding all the day
In the gullies keeping close and out of sight.
But they're watching all the ranges till there's not a bird could fly,
And I'm fairly worn to pieces with the strife,
So I'm taking no more trouble, but I'm going home to die,
'Tis the only way I see to save my life.

'Yes, I'm making home to mother's, and I'll die o' Tuesday next
An' be buried on the Thursday - and, of course,
I'm prepared to meet my penance, but with one thing I'm
    perplexed
And it's - Father, it's this jewel of a horse!
He was never bought nor paid for, and there's not a man can swear
To his owner or his breeder, but I know,
That his sire was by Pedantic from the Old Pretender mare
And his dam was close related to The Roe.

'And there's nothing in the district that can race him for a step,
He could canter while they're going at their top:
He's the king of all the leppers that was ever seen to lep,
A five-foot fence - he'd clear it in a hop!
So I'll leave him with you, Father, till the dead shall rise again,
Tis yourself that knows a good 'un; and, of course,
You can say he's got by Moonlight out of Paddy Murphy's plain
If you're ever asked the breeding of the horse!

'But it's getting on to daylight and it's time to say goodbye,
For the stars above the east are growing pale.
And I'm making home to mother - and it's hard for me to die!
But it's harder still, is keeping out of gaol!
You can ride the old horse over to my grave across the dip
Where the wattle bloom is waving overhead.
Sure he'll jump them fences easy - you must never raise the whip
Or he'll rush 'em! - now, goodbye!' and he had fled!

So they buried Andy Regan, and they buried him to rights,
In the graveyard at the back of Kiley's Hill;
There were five-and-twenty mourners who had five-and-twenty fights
Till the very boldest fighters had their fill.
There were fifty horses racing from the graveyard to the pub,
And their riders flogged each other all the while.
And the lashin's of the liquor! And the lavin's of the grub!
Oh, poor Andy went to rest in proper style.

Then the races came to Kiley's - with a steeplechase and all,
For the folk were mostly Irish round about,
And it takes an Irish rider to be fearless of a fall,
They were training morning in and morning out.
But they never started training till the sun was on the course
For a superstitious story kept 'em back,
That the ghost of Andy Regan on a slashing chestnut horse,
Had been training by the starlight on the track.

And they read the nominations for the races with surprise
And amusement at the Father's little joke,
For a novice had been entered for the steeplechasing prize,
And they found it was Father Riley's moke!
He was neat enough to gallop, he was strong enough to stay!
But his owner's views of training were immense,
For the Reverend Father Riley used to ride him every day,
And he never saw a hurdle nor a fence.

And the priest would join the laughter: 'Oh,' said he, 'I put him in,
For there's five-and-twenty sovereigns to be won.
And the poor would find it useful, if the chestnut chanced to win,
And he'll maybe win when all is said and done!'
He had called him Faugh-a-ballagh, which is French for 'Clear
    the course',
And his colours were a vivid shade of green:
All the Dooleys and O'Donnells were on Father Riley's horse,
While the Orangemen were backing Mandarin!

It was Hogan, the dog poisoner - aged man and very wise,
Who was camping in the racecourse with his swag,
And who ventured the opinion, to the township's great surprise,
That the race would go to Father Riley's nag.
'You can talk about your riders - and the horse has not been schooled,
And the fences is terrific, and the rest!
When the field is fairly going, then ye'll see ye've all been fooled,
And the chestnut horse will battle with the best.

'For there's some has got condition, and they think the race is sure,
And the chestnut horse will fall beneath the weight,
But the hopes of all the helpless, and the prayers of all the poor,
Will be running by his side to keep him straight.
And it's what's the need of schoolin' or of workin' on the track,
Whin the saints are there to guide him round the course!
I've prayed him over every fence - I've prayed him out and back!
And I'll bet my cash on Father Riley's horse!'

Oh, the steeple was a caution! They went tearin' round and round,
And the fences rang and rattled where they struck.
There was some that cleared the water - there was more fell in
   and drowned,
Some blamed the men and others blamed the luck!
But the whips were flying freely when the field came into view,
For the finish down the long green stretch of course,
And in front of all the flyers - jumpin' like a kangaroo,
Came the rank outsider - Father Riley's horse!

Oh, the shouting and the cheering as he rattled past the post!
For he left the others standing, in the straight;
And the rider - well they reckoned it was Andy Regan's ghost,
And it beat 'em how a ghost would draw the weight!
But he weighed in, nine stone seven, then he laughed and disappeared,
Like a banshee (which is Spanish for an elf),
And old Hogan muttered sagely, 'If it wasn't for the beard
They'd be thinking it was Andy Regan's self!'

And the poor of Kiley's Crossing drank the health at Christmastide
Of the chestnut and his rider dressed in green.
There was never such a rider, not since Andy Regan died,
And they wondered who on earth he could have been.
But they settled it among 'em, for the story got about,
'Mongst the bushmen and the people on the course,
That the Devil had been ordered to let Andy Regan out
For the steeplechase on Father Riley's horse!

In the Stable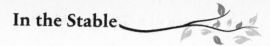

What! you don't like him; well, maybe - we all have our fancies,
   of course:
Brumby to look at, you reckon? Well, no; he's a thoroughbred horse;
Sired by a son of old Panic - look at his ears and his head -
Lop-eared and Roman-nosed, ain't he? - well, that's how the
   Panics are bred.
Gluttonous, ugly and lazy, rough as a tipcart to ride,
Yet if you offered a sovereign apiece for the hairs on his hide
That wouldn't buy him, nor twice that; while I've a pound to
   the good,
This here old stager stays by me and lives like a thoroughbred
should;
Hunt him away from his bedding, and sit yourself down by the wall,
Till you hear how the old fellow saved me from Gilbert,
   O'Meally and Hall.

* * *

Gilbert and Hall and O'Meally, back in the bushranging days,
Made themselves kings of the district - ruled it in old-fashioned ways
Robbing the coach and the escort, stealing our horses at night,
Calling sometimes at the homesteads and giving the women a fright:
Came to the station one morning (and why they did this no
   one knows)
Took a brood mare from the paddock - wanting some fun, I
suppose Fastened a bucket beneath her, hung by a strap around her flank,
Then turned her loose in the timber back of the seven-mile tank.
Go? She went mad! She went tearing and screaming with fear
   through the trees,
While the curst bucket beneath her was banging her flanks
   and her knees.
Bucking and racing and screaming she ran to the back of the run,
Killed herself there in a gully; by God, but they paid for their fun!
Paid for it dear, for the black-boys found tracks, and the
   bucket, and all,

And I swore that I'd live to get even with Gilbert, O'Meally
and Hall.

Day after day then I chased them - 'course they had friends on the sly,
Friends who were willing to sell them to those who were
willing to buy.
Early one morning we found them in camp at the Cockatoo Farm;
One of us shot at O'Meally and wounded him under the arm:
Ran them for miles in the ranges, till Hall, with his horse
fairly beat,
Took to the rocks and we lost him - the others made good
their retreat.

It was war to the knife then, I tell you, and once, on the door
of my shed,
They nailed up a notice that offered a hundred reward for my
head!
Then we heard they were gone from the district; they stuck up
a coach in the West,
And I rode by myself in the paddocks, just taking a bit of a rest,
Riding this colt as a youngster - awkward, half-broken and shy,
He wheeled round one day on a sudden; I looked, but I
couldn't see why -
But I soon found out why, for before me the hillside rose up
like a wall,
And there on the top with their rifles were Gilbert, O'Meally
and Hall!

'Twas a good three-mile run to the homestead - bad going,
with plenty of trees -
So I gathered the youngster together, and gripped at his ribs
with my knees.
'Twas a mighty poor chance to escape them! It puts a man's
nerve to the test
On a half-broken colt to be hunted by the best mounted men
in the West.

But the half-broken colt was a racehorse! He lay down to
   work with a will.
Flashed through the scrub like a clean-skin-by heavens, we
   flew down the hill!
Over a twenty-foot gully he swept with the spring of a deer,
And they fired as we jumped, but they missed me - a bullet
   sang close to my ear -
And the jump gained us ground, for they shirked it: but I saw
   as we raced through the gap
That the rails at the homestead were fastened - I was caught
   like a rat in a trap.
Fenced with barbed wire was the paddock - barbed wire that
   would cut like a knife -
How was a youngster to clear it that never had jumped in his life?

Bang went a rifle behind me - the colt gave a spring, he was hit;
Straight at the sliprails I rode him - I felt him take hold of the bit;
Never a foot to the right or the left did he swerve in his stride,
Awkward and frightened, but honest, the sort it's a pleasure to ride!
Straight at the rails, where they'd fastened barbed wire on the
   top of the post,
Rose like a stag and went over, with hardly a scratch at the most;
Into the homestead I darted, and snatched down my gun
   from the wall,
And I tell you I made them step lively, Gilbert, O'Meally and Hall.

Yes! There's the mark of the bullet - he's got it inside of him yet,
Mixed up somehow with his victuals; but, bless you, he don't
   seem to fret!
Gluttonous, ugly, and lazy - eats anything he can bite;
Now, let us shut up the stable, and bid the old fellow good night.
Ah! we can't breed 'em, the son that were bred when we old
   uns were young....
Yes, as I said, these bushrangers, none of 'em lived to be hung.
Gilbert was shot by the troopers, Hall was betrayed by his friend,
Campbell disposed of O'Meally, bringing the lot to an end.

But you can talk about riding - I've ridden a lot in the past --
Wait till there's rifles behind you, you'll know what it means
    to go fast!
I've steeplechased, raced, and 'run horses', but I think the
    most dashing of all
Was the ride when that old fellow saved me from Gilbert,
O'Meally and Hall!

Old Australian Ways

The London lights are far abeam
Behind a bank of cloud,
Along the shore the gaslights gleam,
The gale is piping loud;
And down the Channel, groping blind,
We drive her through the haze
Towards the land we left behind -
The good old land of 'never mind',
And old Australian ways.

The narrow ways of English folk
Are not for such as we;
They bear the long-accustomed yoke
Of staid conservancy:
But all our roads are new and strange,
And through our blood there runs
The vagabonding love of change
That drove us westward of the range
And westward of the suns.

The city folk go to and fro
Behind a prison's bars,
They never feel the breezes blow
And never see the stars;
They never hear in blossomed trees
The music low and sweet
Of wild birds making melodies,
Nor catch the little laughing breeze
That whispers in the wheat.

Our fathers came of roving stock
That could not fixed abide:
And we have followed field and flock
Since e'er we learnt to ride;
By miner's camp and shearing shed,
In land of heat and drought,
We followed where our fortunes led,
With fortune always on ahead
And always further out.

The wind is in the barley-grass,
The wattles are in bloom;
The breezes greet us as they pass
With honey-sweet perfume;
The parakeets go screaming by
With flash of golden wing,
And from the swamp the wild-ducks cry
Their long-drawn note of revelry,
Rejoicing at the Spring.

So throw the weary pen aside
And let the papers rest,
For we must saddle up and ride
Towards the blue hill's breast;
And we must travel far and fast
Across their rugged maze,
To find the Spring of Youth at last,
And call back from the buried past
The old Australian ways.

When Clancy took the drover's track
In years of long ago,
He drifted to the outer back
Beyond the Overflow;
By rolling plain and rocky shelf,
With stockwhip in his hand,
He reached at last (oh lucky elf!)
The Town of Come-and-help-yourself
In Rough-and-ready Land.

And if it be that you would know
The tracks he used to ride,
Then you must saddle up and go
Beyond the Queensland side -
Beyond the reach of rule or law,
To ride the long day through,
In Nature's homestead - filled with awe
You then might see what Clancy saw
And know what Clancy knew.

We're All Australians Now
(A letter to the troops – 1915)

Australia takes her pen in hand
To write a line to you,
To let you fellows understand
How proud we are of you.

From shearing shed and cattle run,
From Broome to Hobson's Bay,
Each native-born Australian son
Stands straighter up today.

The man who used to 'hump his drum',
On far-out Queensland runs
Is fighting side by side with some
Tasmanian farmer's sons.

The fisher-boys dropped sail and oar
To grimly stand the test,
Along that storm-swept Turkish shore,
With miners from the west.

The old state jealousies of yore
Are dead as Pharaoh's sow,
We're not State children any more -
We're all Australians now!

Our six-starred flag that used to fly
Half-shyly to the breeze,
Unknown where older nations ply
Their trade on foreign seas,

Flies out to meet the morning blue
With Vict'ry at the prow;
For that's the flag the Sydney flew,
The wide seas know it now!

The mettle that a race can show
Is proved with shot and steel,
And now we know what nations know
And feel what nations feel.

The honoured graves beneath the crest
Of Gaba Tepe hill
May hold our bravest and our best,
But we have brave men still.

With all our petty quarrels done,
Dissensions overthrown,
We have, through what you boys have done,
A history of our own.

Our old world diff'rences are dead,
Like weeds beneath the plough,
For English, Scotch, and Irish-bred,
They're all Australians now!

So now we'll toast the Third Brigade
That led Australia's van,
For never shall their glory fade
In minds Australian.

Fight on, fight on, unflinchingly,
Till right and justice reign.
Fight on, fight on, till Victory
Shall send you home again.

And with Australia's flag shall fly
A spray of wattle-bough
To symbolise our unity -
We're all Australians now.

White Cockatoos

Now the autumn maize is growing,
Now the corn-cob fills,
Where the Little River flowing
Winds among the hills.
Over mountain peaks outlying
Clear against the blue
Comes a scout in silence flying,
One white cockatoo.

Back he goes to where the meeting
Waits among the trees.
Says, 'The corn is fit for eating;
Hurry, if you please.'
Skirmishers, their line extending,
Shout the joyful news;
Down they drop like snow descending,
Clouds of cockatoos.

At their husking competition
Hear them screech and yell.
On a gum tree's high position
Sits a sentinel.
Soon the boss goes boundary riding;
But the wise old bird,
Mute among the branches hiding,
Never says a word.

Then you hear the strident squalling:
'Here's the boss's son,
Through the garden bushes crawling,
Crawling with a gun.
May the shiny cactus bristles
Fill his soul with woe;
May his knees get full of thistles.
Brothers, let us go.'

Old Black Harry sees them going,
Sketches Nature's plan:
'That one cocky too much knowing,
All same Chinaman.
One eye shut and one eye winkin' -
Never shut the two;
Chinaman go dead, me thinkin',
Jump up cockatoo.'

A Bush Christening

On the outer Barcoo where the churches are few,
And men of religion are scanty,
On a road never cross'd 'cept by folk that are lost,
One Michael Magee had a shanty.

Now this Mike was the dad of a ten-year-old lad,
Plump, healthy, and stoutly conditioned;
He was strong as the best, but poor Mike had no rest
For the youngster had never been christened.

And his wife used to cry, 'If the darlin' should die
Saint Peter would not recognize him.'
But by luck he survived till a preacher arrived,
Who agreed straightaway to baptize him.

Now the artful young rogue, while they held their collogue,
With his ear to the keyhole was listenin';
And he muttered in fright, while his features turned white,
What the divil and all is this christenin'?'

He was none of your dolts - He had seen them brand colts,
And it seemed to his small understanding,
If the man in the frock made him one of the flock,
It must mean something very like branding.

So away with a rush he set off for the bush,
While the tears in his eyelids they glistened -
"Tis outrageous,' says he, 'to brand youngsters like me;
I'll be dashed if I'll stop to be christened!'

Like a young native dog he ran into a log,
And his father with language uncivil,
Never heeding the 'praste', cried aloud in his haste
'Come out and be christened, you divil!'

But he lay there as snug as a bug in a rug,
And his parents in vain might reprove him,
Till his reverence spoke (he was fond of a joke)
'I've a notion,' says he, 'that'll move him.

'Poke a stick up the log, give the spalpeen a prog;
Poke him aisy - don't hurt him or maim him;
'Tis not long that he'll stand, I've the water at hand,
As he rushes out this end I'll name him.

'Here he comes, and for shame, ye've forgotten the name --
Is it Patsy or Michael or Dinnis?'
Here the youngster ran out, and the priest gave a shout --
'Take your chance, anyhow, wid `Maginnis'!'

As the howling young cub ran away to the scrub
Where he knew that pursuit would be risky,
The priest, as he fled, flung a flask at his head
That was labelled 'Maginnis's Whisky'!

Now Maginnis Magee has been made a J.P.,
And the one thing he hates more than sin is
To be asked by the folk, who have heard of the joke,
How he came to be christened Maginnis!

Under the Shadow of Kiley's Hill

This is the place where they all were bred;
Some of the rafters are standing still;
Now they are scattered and lost and dead,
Every one from the old nest fled,
Out of the shadow of Kiley's Hill.

Better it is that they ne'er came back -
Changes and chances are quickly rung;
Now the old homestead is gone to rack,
Green is the grass on the well-worn track
Down by the gate where the roses clung.

Gone is the garden they kept with care;
Left to decay at its own sweet will,
Fruit trees and flower-beds eaten bare,
Cattle and sheep where the roses were,
Under the shadow of Kiley's Hill.

Where are the children that strove and grew
In the old homestead in days gone by?
One is away on the far Barcoo
Watching his cattle the long year through,
Watching them starve in the droughts and die.

One, in the town where all cares are rife,
Weary with troubles that cramp and kill,
Fain would be done with the restless strife,
Fain would go back to the old bush life,
Back to the shadow of Kiley's Hill.

One is away on the roving quest,
Seeking his share of the golden spoil;
Out in the wastes of the trackless west,
Wandering ever he gives the best
Of his years and strength to the hopeless toil.

What of the parents? That unkempt mound
Shows where they slumber united still;
Rough is their grave, but they sleep as sound
Out on the range as in holy ground,
Under the shadow of Kiley's Hill.

Brumby's Run

[*The Aboriginal word for a wild horse is 'brumby.*
At a trial a judge asked 'Who is Brumby and
where is his Run?' This inspired the following
poem.]

It lies beyond the Western Pines
Towards the sinking sun,
And not a survey mark defines
The bounds of 'Brumby's Run'.

On odds and ends of mountain land
On tracks of range and rock
Where no one else can make a stand,
Old Brumby rears his stock.

A wild, unhandled lot they are
Of every shape and breed,
They venture out 'neath moon and star
Along the flats to feed;

But when the dawn makes pink the sky
And steals along the plain,
The Brumby horses turn and fly
Towards the hills again.

The traveller by the mountain-track
May hear their hoof-beats pass,
And catch a glimpse of brown and black,
Dim shadows on the grass.

The eager stock horse pricks his ears
And lifts his head on high
In wild excitement when he hears
The Brumby mob go by.

Old Brumby asks no price or fee
O'er all his wide domains:
The man who yards his stock is free
To keep them for his pains.

So, off to scour the mountainside
With eager eyes aglow,
To strongholds where the wild mobs hide
The gully-rakers go.

A rush of horses through the trees,
A red shirt making play;
The sound of stockwhips on the breeze,
They vanish far away!

* * *

Ah, me! before our day is done
We long with bitter pain
To ride once more on Brumby's Run
And yard his mob again.

A Singer of the Bush

There is waving of grass in the breeze
   And a song in the air,
And a murmur of myriad bees
   That toil everywhere.
There is scent in the blossom and bough,
   And the breath of the Spring
Is as soft as a kiss on a brow —
   And Spring-time I sing.

There is drought on the land, and the stock
   Tumble down in their tracks
Or follow — a tottering flock —
   The scrub-cutter's axe.
While ever a creature survives
   The axes shall swing;
We are fighting with fate for their lives —
   And the combat I sing.

Pioneers

They came of bold and roving stock that would not fixed abide;
They were the sons of field and flock since e'er they learnt to ride,
We may not hope to see such men in these degenerate years
As those explorers of the bush — the brave old pioneers.

'Twas they who rode the trackless bush in heat and storm and drought;
'Twas they who heard the master-word that called them farther out;
'Twas they who followed up the trail the mountain cattle made,
And pressed across the mighty range where now their bones are laid.

But now the times are dull and slow, the brave old days are dead
When hardy bushmen started out, and forced their way ahead
By tangled scrub and forests grim towards the unknown west,
And spied the far-off promised land from off the range's crest.

Oh! ye that sleep in lonely graves by far-off ridge and plain,
We drink to you in silence now as Christmas comes again,
To you who fought the wilderness through rough unsettled years —
The founders of our nation's life, the brave old pioneers.

Flying Squirrels

On the rugged water shed
At the top of the bridle track
Where years ago, as the old men say,
The splitters went with a bullock dray
But never a dray came back;

At the time of the gum tree bloom,
When the scent in the air is strong,
And the blossom stirs in the evening breeze,
You may see the squirrels among the trees,
Playing the whole night long.

Never a care at all
Bothers their simple brains;
You can see them glide in the moonlight dim
From tree to tree and from limb to limb,
Little grey aeroplanes.

Each like a dormouse sleeps
In the spout of a gumtree old,
A ball of fur with a silver coat;
Each with his tail around his throat
For fear of his catching cold.

These are the things he eats,
Asking his friends to dine:
Moths and beetles and newborn shoots,
Honey and snacks of the native fruits,
And a glass of dew for wine.

The Weather Prophet

"Ow can it rain," the old man said, "with things the way they are?
You've got to learn off ant and bee, and jackass and galah;
And no man never saw it rain, for fifty years at least,
Not when the blessed parakeets are flyin' to the east!"

The weeks went by, the squatter wrote to tell his bank the news.
"It's still as dry as dust," he said, "I'm feeding all the ewes;
The overdraft would sink a ship, but make your mind at rest,
It's all right now, the parakeets are flyin' to the west."

Australian Scenery

The Mountains

A land of sombre, silent hills, where mountain cattle go
By twisted tracks, on sidelings steep, where giant gumtrees grow
And the wind replies, in the river oaks, to the song of the
stream below.

A land where the hills keep watch and ward, silent and wide awake
As those who sit by a dead campfire, and wait for the dawn to break,
Or those who watched by the Holy Cross for the dead
Redeemer's sake.

A land where silence lies so deep that sound itself is dead
And a gaunt grey bird, like a homeless soul, drifts, noiseless, overhead
And the world's great story is left untold, and the message is
left unsaid.

The Plains

A land, as far as the eye can see, where the waving grasses grow
Or the plains are blackened and burnt and bare, where the
false mirages go
Like shifting symbols of hope deferred — land where you
never know.

Land of plenty or land of want, where the grey Companions dance,
Feast or famine, or hope or fear, and in all things land of chance,
Where Nature pampers or Nature slays, in her ruthless red,
romance.

And we catch a sound of a fairy's song, as the wind goes
whipping by,
Or a scent like incense drifts along from the herbage ripe and dry
— Or the dust storms dance on their ballroom floor, where
the bones of the cattle lie.

Sunrise on the Coast

Grey dawn on the sandhills — the night wind has drifted
  All night from the rollers a scent of the sea;
With the dawn the grey fog his battalions has lifted,
  At the scent of the morning they scatter and flee.

Like mariners calling the roll of their number
  The sea fowl put out to the infinite deep.
And far overhead — sinking softly to slumber —
  Worn out by their watching, the stars fall asleep.

To eastward where resteth the dome of the skies on
  The sea line stirs softly the curtain of night;
And far from behind the enshrouded horizon
  Comes the voice of a God saying, "Let there be light."

An lo, there is light! Evanescent and tender,
  It glows ruby-red where 'twas now ashen grey;
And purple and scarlet and gold in its splendour —
  Behold, 'tis that marvel, the birth of a day!

At the Melting of the Snow

There's a sunny Southern land,
  And it's there that I would be
Where the big hills stand,
  In the South Countrie!
When the wattles bloom again,
  Then it's time for us to go
To the old Monaro country
  At the melting of the snow.

To the East or to the West,
  Or wherever you may be,
You will find no place
  Like the South Countrie.
For the skies are blue above,
  And the grass is green below,
In the old Monaro country
  At the melting of the snow.

Now the team is in the plough,
  And the thrushes start to sing,
And the pigeons on the bough
  Sit a-welcoming the Spring.
So come my comrades all,
  Let us saddle up and go
To the old Monaro country
  At the melting of the snow.

The Travelling Post Office

The roving breezes come and go, the reed beds sweep and
sway,
The sleepy river murmurs low, and loiters on its way,
It is the land of lots o' time along the Castlereagh.

The old man's son had left the farm, he found it dull and
slow,
He drifted to the great North-west where all the rovers go.
"He's gone so long," the old man said, "he's dropped right out of
mind,
But if you'd write a line to him I'd take it very kind;
He's shearing here and fencing there, a kind of waif and stray,
He's droving now with Conroy's sheep along the Castlereagh.
The sheep are travelling for the grass, and travelling very slow;
They may be at Mundooran now, or past the Overflow,
Or tramping down the black soil flats across by Waddiwong,
But all those little country towns would send the letter wrong,
The mailman, if he's extra tired, would pass them in his sleep,
It's safest to address the note to 'Care of Conroy's sheep',
For five and twenty thousand head can scarcely go astray,
You write to 'Care of Conroy's sheep along the Castlereagh'."

By rock and ridge and riverside the western mail has gone,
Across the great Blue Mountain Range to take that letter on.
A moment on the topmost grade while open fire doors glare,
She pauses like a living thing to breathe the mountain air,
Then launches down the other side across the plains away
To bear that note to "Conroy's sheep along the Castlereagh".

And now by coach and mailman's bag it goes from town to town,
And Conroy's Gap and Conroy's Creek have marked it
"further down".
Beneath a sky of deepest blue where never cloud abides,
A speck upon the waste of plain the lonely mailman rides.

Where fierce hot winds have set the pine and myall boughs asweep.
He hails the shearers passing by for news of Conroy's sheep.
By big lagoons where wildfowl play and crested pigeons flock,

By camp fires where the drovers ride around their restless stock,
And past the teamster toiling down to fetch the wool away
My letter chases Conroy's sheep along the Castlereagh.

Come-by-Chance

As I pondered very weary o'er a volume long and dreary —
For the plot was void of interest; 'twas the Postal Guide, in fact —
There I learnt the true location, distance, size and population
Of each township, town, and village in the radius of the Act.
And I learnt that Puckawidgee stands beside the Murrumbidgee,
And the Booleroi and Bumble get their letters twice a year,
Also that the post inspector, when he visited Collector,
Closed the office up instanter, and re-opened Dungalear.

But my languid mood forsook me, when I found a name that took me;
Quite by chance I came across it — "Come-by-Chance" was
what I read;
No location was assigned it, not a thing to help one find it,
Just an N which stood for northward, and the rest was all unsaid.

I shall leave my home, and forthward wander stoutly to the northward
Till I come by chance across it, and I'll straightway settle down;
For there can't be any hurry, nor the slightest cause for worry
Where the telegraph don't reach you nor the railways run to town.

And one's letters and exchanges come by chance across the ranges,
Where a wiry young Australian leads a packhorse once a week,
And the good news grows by keeping, and you're spared the
pain of weeping
Over bad news when the mailman drops the letters in a creek.

But I fear, and more's the pity, that there's really no such city,
For there's not a man can find it of the shrewdest folk I know;
"Come-by-Chance", be sure it never means a land of fierce
endeavour —
It is just the careless country where the dreamers only go.

*   *   *   *   *   *   *

Though we work and toil and hustle in our life of haste and bustle,
All that makes our life worth living comes unstriven for and free;
Man may weary and importune, but the fickle goddess Fortune
Deals him out his pain or pleasure, careless what his worth
may be.

All the happy times entrancing, days of sport and nights of dancing,
Moonlit rides and stolen kisses, pouting lips and loving glance:
When you think of these be certain you have looked behind
the curtain,
You have had the luck to linger just a while in "Come-by-Chance".

By the Grey Gulf-Water

Far to the Northward there lies a land,
  A wonderful land that the winds blow over,
And none may fathom nor understand
  The charm it holds for the restless rover;
A great grey chaos — a land half made,
  Where endless space is and no life stirreth;
And the soul of a man will recoil afraid
  From the sphinx-like visage that Nature weareth.
But old Dame Nature, though scornful, craves
  Her dole of death and her share of slaughter;
Many indeed are the nameless graves
  Where her victims sleep by the Grey Gulf-water.

Slowly and slowly those grey streams glide,
  Drifting along with a languid motion,
Lapping the reed-beds on either side,
  Wending their way to the Northern Ocean.
Grey are the plains where the emus pass
  Silent and slow, with their staid demeanour;
Over the dead men's graves the grass
  Maybe is waving a trifle greener.
Down in the world where men toil and spin
  Dame Nature smiles as man's hand has taught her;
Only the dead men her smiles can win
  In the great lone land by the Grey Gulf-water.

For the strength of man is an insect's strength
  In the face of that mighty plain and river,
And the life of a man is a moment's length
  To the life of the stream that will run for ever.
And so it cometh they take no part
  In small-world worries; each hardy rover
Rideth abroad and is light of heart,
  With the plains around and the blue sky over.
And up in the heavens the brown lark sings
  The songs that the strange wild land has taught her;
Full of thanksgiving her sweet song rings —
  And I wish I were back by the Grey Gulf-water.

A Voice from the Town

I thought, in the days of the droving,
Of steps I might hope to retrace,
To be done with the bush and the roving
And settle once more in my place.
With a heart that was well nigh to breaking,
In the long, lonely rides on the plain,
I thought of the pleasure of taking
The hand of a lady again.

I am back into civilization,
Once more in the stir and the strife,
But the old joys have lost their sensation —
The light has gone out of my life;
The men of my time they have married,
Made fortunes or gone to the wall;
Too long from the scene I have tarried,
And somehow, I'm out of it all.

For I go to the balls and the races
A lonely companionless elf,
And the ladies bestow all their graces
On others less grey than myself;
While the talk goes around I'm a dumb one
'Midst youngsters that chatter and prate,
And they call me "The Man who was Someone
Way back in the year Sixty-eight."

And I look, sour and old, at the dancers
That swing to the strains of the band,
And the ladies all give me the Lancers,
No waltzes — I quite understand.
For matrons intent upon matching
Their daughters with infinite push,
Would scarce think him worthy the catching,
The broken-down man from the bush.

New partners have come and new faces,
And I, of the bygone brigade,
Sharply feel that oblivion my place is —
I must lie with the rest in the shade.
And the youngsters, fresh-featured and pleasant,
They live as we lived — fairly fast;
But I doubt if the men of the present
Are as good as the men of the past.

Of excitement and praise they are chary,
There is nothing much good upon earth;
Their watchword is nil admirari,
They are bored from the days of their birth.
Where the life that we led was a revel
They "wince and relent and refrain" —
I could show them the road — to the devil,
Were I only a youngster again.

I could show them the road where the stumps are,
The pleasures that end in remorse,
And the game where the Devil's three trumps are
The woman, the card, and the horse.
Shall the blind lead the blind — shall the sower
Of wind read the storm as of yore?
Though they get to their goal somewhat slower,
They march where we hurried before.

For the world never learns — just as we did
They gallantly go to their fate,
Unheeded all warnings, unheeded
The maxims of elders sedate.
As the husbandman, patiently toiling,
Draws a harvest each year from the soil,
So the fools grow afresh for the spoiling,
And a new crop of thieves for the spoil.

But a truce to this dull moralizing,
Let them drink while the drops are of gold.
I have tasted the dregs — 'twere surprising
Were the new wine to me like the old;
And I weary for lack of employment
In idleness day after day,
For the key to the door of enjoyment
Is Youth — and I've thrown it away.

With the Cattle

The drought is down on field and flock,
  The river-bed is dry;
And we must shift the starving stock
  Before the cattle die.
We muster up with weary hearts
  At breaking of the day,
And turn our heads to foreign parts,
  To take the stock away.
    And it's hunt 'em up and dog 'em,
    And it's get the whip and flog 'em,
For it's weary work is droving when they're dying every day;
    By stock-routes bare and eaten,
    On dusty roads and beaten,
With half a chance to save their lives we take the stock away.

We cannot use the whip for shame
  On beasts that crawl along;
We have to drop the weak and lame,
  And try to save the strong;
The wrath of God is on the track,
  The drought fiend holds his sway,
With blows and cries and stockwhip crack
  We take the stock away.
    As they fall we leave them lying,
    With the crows to watch them dying,
Grim sextons of the Overland that fasten on their prey;
    By the fiery dust-storm drifting,
    And the mocking mirage shifting,
In heat and drought and hopeless pain we take the stock away.

In dull despair the days go by
  With never hope of change,
But every stage we draw more nigh
  Towards the mountain range;

And some may live to climb the pass,
  And reach the great plateau,
And revel in the mountain grass,
  By streamlets fed with snow.
    As the mountain wind is blowing
    It starts the cattle lowing,
And calling to each other down the dusty long array;
    And there speaks a grizzled drover:
    "Well, thank God, the worst is over,
The creatures smell the mountain grass that's twenty miles
away."

They press towards the mountain grass,
  They look with eager eyes
Along the rugged stony pass,
  That slopes towards the skies;
Their feet may bleed from rocks and stones,
  But though the blood-drop starts,
They struggle on with stifled groans,
  For hope is in their hearts.
    And the cattle that are leading,
    Though their feet are worn and bleeding,
Are breaking to a kind of run — pull up, and let them go!
    For the mountain wind is blowing,
    And the mountain grass is growing,
They settle down by running streams ice-cold with melted snow.

. . . . . .

The days are done of heat and drought
  Upon the stricken plain;
The wind has shifted right about,
  And brought the welcome rain;
The river runs with sullen roar,
  All flecked with yellow foam,
And we must take the road once more,
  To bring the cattle home.

And it's "Lads! we'll raise a chorus,
   There's a pleasant trip before us."
And the horses bound beneath us as we start them down the
track;
   And the drovers canter, singing,
   Through the sweet green grasses springing,
Towards the far-off mountain-land, to bring the cattle back.

Are these the beasts we brought away
  That move so lively now?
They scatter off like flying spray
  Across the mountain's brow;
And dashing down the rugged range
  We hear the stockwhip crack,
Good faith, it is a welcome change
  To bring such cattle back.
   And it's "Steady down the lead there!"
   And it's "Let 'em stop and feed there!"
For they're wild as mountain eagles and their sides are all
afoam;
   But they're settling down already,
   And they'll travel nice and steady,
With cheery call and jest and song we fetch the cattle home.

We have to watch them close at night
  For fear they'll make a rush,
And break away in headlong flight
  Across the open bush;
And by the camp-fire's cheery blaze,
  With mellow voice and strong,
We hear the lonely watchman raise
  The Overlander's song:
   "Oh! it's when we're done with roving,
   With the camping and the droving,
It's homeward down the Bland we'll go, and never more we'll roam;"
   While the stars shine out above us,
   Like the eyes of those who love us —
The eyes of those who watch and wait to greet the cattle home.

The plains are all awave with grass,
  The skies are deepest blue;
And leisurely the cattle pass
  And feed the long day through;
But when we sight the station gate,
  We make the stockwhips crack,
A welcome sound to those who wait
  To greet the cattle back:
    And through the twilight falling
    We hear their voices calling,
As the cattle splash across the ford and churn it into foam;
    And the children run to meet us,
    And our wives and sweethearts greet us,
Their heroes from the Overland who brought the cattle home.

Our New Horse

The boys had come back from the races
All silent and down on their luck;
They'd backed 'em, straight out and for places,
But never a winner they'd struck.
They lost their good money on Slogan,
And fell most uncommonly flat
When Partner, the pride of the Bogan,
Was beaten by Aristocrat.

And one said, "I move that instanter
We sell out our horses and quit;
The brutes ought to win in a canter,
Such trials they do when they're fit.
The last one they ran was a snorter —
A gallop to gladden one's heart —
Two-twelve for a mile and a quarter,
And finished as straight as a dart.

"And then when I think that they're ready
To win me a nice little swag,
They are licked like the veriest neddy —
They're licked from the fall of the flag.
The mare held her own to the stable,
She died out to nothing at that,
And Partner he never seemed able
To pace with the Aristocrat.

"And times have been bad, and the seasons
Don't promise to be of the best;
In short, boys, there's plenty of reasons
For giving the racing a rest.
The mare can be kept on the station —
Her breeding is good as can be —
But Partner, his next destination
Is rather a trouble to me.

"We can't sell him here, for they know him
As well as the clerk of the course;
He's raced and won races till, blow him,
He's done as a handicap horse.
A jady, uncertain performer,
They weight him right out of the hunt,
And clap it on warmer and warmer
Whenever he gets near the front.

"It's no use to paint him or dot him
Or put any fake on his brand,
For bushmen are smart, and they'd spot him
In any sale-yard in the land.
The folk about here could all tell him,
Could swear to each separate hair;
Let us send him to Sydney and sell him,
There's plenty of Jugginses there.

"We'll call him a maiden, and treat 'em
To trials will open their eyes;
We'll run their best horses and beat 'em,
And then won't they think him a prize.
I pity the fellow that buys him,
He'll find in a very short space,
No matter how highly he tries him,
The beggar won't race in a race."

*　　*　　*　　*　　*

Next week, under "Seller and Buyer",
Appeared in the Daily Gazette:
"A racehorse for sale, and a flyer;
Has never been started as yet;
A trial will show what his pace is;
The buyer can get him in light,
And win all the handicap races.
Apply before Saturday night."

He sold for a hundred and thirty,
Because of a gallop he had
One morning with Bluefish and Bertie.
And donkey-licked both of 'em bad.
And when the old horse had departed,
The life on the station grew tame;
The race-track was dull and deserted,
The boys had gone back on the game.

                  *   *   *   *   *

The winter rolled by, and the station
Was green with the garland of Spring;
A spirit of glad exultation
Awoke in each animate thing;
And all the old love, the old longing,
Broke out in the breasts of the boys —
The visions of racing came thronging
With all its delirious joys.

The rushing of floods in their courses,
The rattle of rain on the roofs,
Recalled the fierce rush of the horses,
The thunder of galloping hoofs.
And soon one broke out: "I can suffer
No longer the life of a slug;
The man that don't race is a duffer,
Let's have one more run for the mug.

"Why, everything races, no matter
Whatever its method may be:
The waterfowl hold a regatta;
The possums run heats up a tree;
The emus are constantly sprinting
A handicap out on the plain;
It seems that all nature is hinting
'Tis time to be at it again.

"The cockatoo parrots are talking
Of races to far-away lands;
The native companions are walking
A go-as-you-please on the sands;
The little foals gallop for pastime;
The wallabies race down the gap;
Let's try it once more for the last time —
Bring out the old jacket and cap.

"And now for a horse; we might try one
Of those that are bred on the place.
But I fancy it's better to buy one,
A horse that has proved he can race.
Let us send down to Sydney to Skinner,
A thorough good judge who can ride,
And ask him to buy us a spinner
To clean out the whole country-side."

They wrote him a letter as follows:
"We want you to buy us a horse;
He must have the speed to catch swallows,
And stamina with it, of course.
The price ain't a thing that'll grieve us,
It's getting a bad un annoys
The undersigned blokes, and believe us,
We're yours to a cinder, 'the boys'."

He answered: "I've bought you a hummer,
A horse that has never been raced;
I saw him run over the Drummer,
He held him outclassed and outpaced.
His breeding's not known, but they state he
Is born of a thoroughbred strain.
I've paid them a hundred and eighty,
And started the horse in the train."

They met him — alas, that these verses
Aren't up to their subject's demands,
Can't set forth their eloquent curses —
For Partner was back in their hands.
They went in to meet him with gladness
They opened his box with delight —
A silent procession of sadness
They crept to the station at night.

And life has grown dull on the station,
The boys are all silent and slow;
Their work is a daily vexation,
And sport is unknown to them now.
Whenever they think how they stranded,
They squeal just as guinea-pigs squeal;
They'd bit their own hook, and were landed
With fifty pounds loss on the deal.

Do They Know?

Do they know? At the turn of the straight
    Where the favourites fail,
And every atom of weight
    Is telling its tale;
As some grim old stayer hard-pressed
    Runs true to his breed
And with head just in front of the rest
    Fights on in the lead;
When the jockeys are out with the whips
    With a furlong to go;
And the backers grow white to the lips
    Do you think *they* don't know?

Do they know? As they come back to weigh
    In a whirlwind of cheers,
Though the spurs have left marks of the fray,
    Though the sweat on their ears
Gathers cold, and they sob with distress
    As they roll up the track,
They know just as well their success
    As the man on their back.
As they walk through a dense human lane
    That sways to and fro
And cheers them again and again,
    Do you think *they* don't know?

The Wind's Message

There came a whisper down the Bland between the dawn and dark,
Above the tossing of the pines, above the river's flow;
It stirred the boughs of giant gums and stalwart ironbark;
It drifted where the wild ducks played amid the swamps below;
It brought a breath of mountain air from off the hills of pine,
A scent of eucalyptus trees in honey-laden bloom;
And drifting, drifting far away along the southern line
It caught from leaf and grass and fern a subtle strange perfume.

It reached the toiling city folk, but few there were that heard —
The rattle of their busy life had choked the whisper down;
And some but caught a fresh-blown breeze with scent of pine that stirred
A thought of blue hills far away beyond the smoky town;
And others heard the whisper pass, but could not understand
The magic of the breeze's breath that set their hearts aglow,
Nor how the roving wind could bring across the Overland
A sound of voices silent now and songs of long ago.

But some that heard the whisper clear were filled with vague unrest;
The breeze had brought its message home, they could not fixed abide;
Their fancies wandered all the day towards the blue hills' breast,
Towards the sunny slopes that lie along the riverside,
The mighty rolling western plains are very fair to see,
Where waving to the passing breeze the silver myalls stand,
But fairer are the giant hills, all rugged though they be,
From which the two great rivers rise that run along the Bland.

Oh! rocky range and rugged spur and river running clear,
That swings around the sudden bends with swirl of snow-
white foam,
Though we, your sons, are far away, we sometimes seem to hear
The message that the breezes bring to call the wanderers home.
The mountain peaks are white with snow that feeds a
thousand rills,
Along the river banks the maize grows tall on virgin land,
And we shall live to see once more those sunny southern hills,
And strike once more the bridle track that leads along the Bland.

How Gilbert Died

There's never a stone at the sleeper's head,
There's never a fence beside,
And the wandering stock on the grave may tread
Unnoticed and undenied;
But the smallest child on the Watershed
Can tell you how Gilbert died.
For he rode at dusk with his comrade Dunn
To the hut at the Stockman's Ford;
In the waning light of the sinking sun
They peered with a fierce accord.
They were outlaws both — and on each man's head
Was a thousand pounds reward.

They had taken toll of the country round,
And the troopers came behind
With a black who tracked like a human hound
In the scrub and the ranges blind:
He could run the trail where a white man's eye
No sign of track could find.

He had hunted them out of the One Tree Hill
And over the Old Man Plain,
But they wheeled their tracks with a wild beast's skill,
And they made for the range again;
Then away to the hut where their grandsire dwelt
They rode with a loosened rein.

And their grandsire gave them a greeting bold:
"Come in and rest in peace,
No safer place does the country hold —
With the night pursuit must cease,
And we'll drink success to the roving boys,
And to hell with the black police."

But they went to death when they entered there
In the hut at the Stockman's Ford,
For their grandsire's words were as false as fair —
They were doomed to the hangman's cord.
He had sold them both to the black police
For the sake of the big reward.

In the depth of night there are forms that glide
As stealthily as serpents creep,
And around the hut where the outlaws hide
They plant in the shadows deep,
And they wait till the first faint flush of dawn
Shall waken their prey from sleep.

But Gilbert wakes while the night is dark —
A restless sleeper aye.
He has heard the sound of a sheep-dog's bark,
And his horse's warning neigh,
And he says to his mate, "There are hawks abroad,
And it's time that we went away."

Their rifles stood at the stretcher head,
Their bridles lay to hand;
They wakened the old man out of his bed,
When they heard the sharp command:
"In the name of the Queen lay down your arms,
Now, Dun and Gilbert, stand!"

Then Gilbert reached for his rifle true
That close at hand he kept;
He pointed straight at the voice, and drew,
But never a flash outleapt,
For the water ran from the rifle breech —
It was drenched while the outlaws slept.

Then he dropped the piece with a bitter oath,
And he turned to his comrade Dunn:
"We are sold," he said, "we are dead men both! —
Still, there may be a chance for one;
I'll stop and I'll fight with the pistol here,
You take to your heels and run."

So Dunn crept out on his hands and knees
In the dim, half-dawning light,
And he made his way to a patch of trees,
And was lost in the black of night;
And the trackers hunted his tracks all day,
But they never could trace his flight.

But Gilbert walked from the open door
In a confident style and rash;
He heard at his side the rifles roar,
And he heard the bullets crash.
But he laughed as he lifted his pistol-hand,
And he fired at the rifle-flash.

Then out of the shadows the troopers aimed
At his voice and the pistol sound.
With rifle flashes the darkness flamed —
He staggered and spun around,
And they riddled his body with rifle balls
As it lay on the blood-soaked ground.
There's never a stone at the sleeper's head,
There's never a fence beside,
And the wandering stock on the grave may tread
Unnoticed and undenied;
But the smallest child on the Watershed
Can tell you how Gilbert died.

Boots

We've travelled per Joe Gardiner, a humping of our swag
In the country of the Gidgee and Belar.
We've swum the Di'mantina with our raiment in a bag,
And we've travelled per superior motor car,
But when we went to Germany we hadn't any choice,
No matter what our training or pursuits,
For they gave us no selection 'twixt a Ford or Rolls de Royce
So we did it in our good Australian boots.

They called us "mad Australians"; they couldn't understand
How officers and men could fraternise,
They said that we were "reckless", we were "wild, and out of hand",
With nothing great or sacred to our eyes.
But on one thing you could gamble, in the thickest of the fray,
Though they called us volunteers and raw recruits,
You could track us past the shell holes, and the tracks were all one way
Of the good Australian ammunition boots.

The Highlanders were next of kin, the Irish were a treat,
The Yankees knew it all and had to learn,
The Frenchmen kept it going, both in vict'ry and defeat,
Fighting grimly till the tide was on the turn.
And our army kept beside 'em, did its bit and took its chance,
And I hailed our newborn nation and its fruits,
As I listened to the clatter on the cobblestones of France
Of the good Australian military boots.

Black Swans

As I lie at rest on a patch of clover
In the Western Park when the day is done,
I watch as the wild black swans fly over
With their phalanx turned to the sinking sun;
And I hear the clang of their leader crying
To a lagging mate in the rearward flying,
And they fade away in the darkness dying,
Where the stars are mustering one by one.

Oh! ye wild black swans, 'twere a world of wonder
For a while to join in your westward flight,
With the stars above and the dim earth under,
Through the cooling air of the glorious night.
As we swept along on our pinions winging,
We should catch the chime of a church-bell ringing,
Or the distant note of a torrent singing,
Or the far-off flash of a station light.

From the northern lakes with the reeds and rushes,
Where the hills are clothed with a purple haze,
Where the bell-birds chime and the songs of thrushes
Make music sweet in the jungle maze,
They will hold their course to the westward ever,
Till they reach the banks of the old grey river,
Where the waters wash, and the reed-beds quiver
In the burning heat of the summer days.

Oh! ye strange wild birds, will ye bear a greeting
To the folk that live in that western land?
Then for every sweep of your pinions beating,
Ye shall bear a wish to the sunburnt band,
To the stalwart men who are stoutly fighting
With the heat and drought and the dust-storm smiting,
Yet whose life somehow has a strange inviting,
When once to the work they have put their hand.

Facing it yet! Oh, my friend stout-hearted,
What does it matter for rain or shine,
For the hopes deferred and the gain departed?
Nothing could conquer that heart of thine.
And thy health and strength are beyond confessing
As the only joys that are worth possessing.
May the days to come be as rich in blessing
As the days we spent in the auld lang syne.

I would fain go back to the old grey river,
To the old bush days when our hearts were light,
But, alas! those days they have fled for ever,
They are like the swans that have swept from sight.
And I know full well that the strangers' faces
Would meet us now in our dearest places;
For our day is dead and has left no traces
But the thoughts that live in my mind to-night.

There are folk long dead, and our hearts would sicken —
We would grieve for them with a bitter pain,
If the past could live and the dead could quicken,
We then might turn to that life again.
But on lonely nights we would hear them calling,
We should hear their steps on the pathways falling,
We should loathe the life with a hate appalling
In our lonely rides by the ridge and plain.

In the silent park is a scent of clover,
And the distant roar of the town is dead,
And I hear once more as the swans fly over
Their far-off clamour from overhead.
They are flying west, by their instinct guided,
And for man likewise is his fate decided,
And griefs apportioned and joys divided
By a mighty power with a purpose dread.

A Mountain Station

I bought a run a while ago,
  On country rough and ridgy,
Where wallaroos and wombats grow —
  The Upper Murrumbidgee.
The grass is rather scant, it's true,
  But this a fair exchange is,
The sheep can see a lovely view
  By climbing up the ranges.

And She-oak Flat's the station's name,
  I'm not surprised at that, sirs:
The oaks were there before I came,
  And I supplied the flat, sirs.
A man would wonder how it's done,
  The stock so soon decreases —
They sometimes tumble off the run
  And break themselves to pieces.

I've tried to make expenses meet,
  But wasted all my labours,
The sheep the dingoes didn't eat
  Were stolen by the neighbours.
They stole my pears — my native pears —
  Those thrice-convicted felons,
And ravished from me unawares
  My crop of paddy-melons.

And sometimes under sunny skies,
  Without an explanation,
The Murrumbidgee used to rise
  And overflow the station.
But this was caused (as now I know)
  When summer sunshine glowing
Had melted all Kiandra's snow
  And set the river going.

And in the news, perhaps you read:
  "Stock passings. Puckawidgee,
Fat cattle: Seven hundred head
  Swept down the Murrumbidgee;
Their destination's quite obscure,
  But, somehow, there's a notion,
Unless the river falls, they're sure
  To reach the Southern Ocean."

So after that I'll give it best;
  No more with Fate I'll battle.
I'll let the river take the rest,
  For those were all my cattle.
And with one comprehensive curse
  I close my brief narration,
And advertise it in my verse —
  "For Sale! A Mountain Station."

Those Names

The shearers sat in the firelight, hearty and hale and strong,
After the hard day's shearing, passing the joke along:
The "ringer" that shore a hundred, as they never were shorn before,
And the novice who, toiling bravely, had tommy-hawked half a score,
The tarboy, the cook and the skushy, the sweeper that swept the board,
The picker-up, and the penner, with the rest of the shearing horde.
There were men from the inland stations where the skies like a furnace glow,
And men from Snowy River, the land of frozen snow;
There were swarthy Queensland drovers who reckoned all land by miles,
And farmers' sons from the Murray, where many a vineyard smiles.
They started at telling stories when they wearied of cards and games,
And to give these stories flavour they threw in some local names,

Then a man from the bleak Monaro, away on the tableland,
He fixed his eyes on the ceiling, and he started to play his hand.
He told them of Adjintoothbong, where the pine-clad mountains freeze,
And the weight of the snow in summer breaks branches off the trees,
And, as he warmed to the business, he let them have it strong —
Nimitybelle, Conargo, Wheeo, Bongongolong;
He lingered over them fondly, because they recalled to mind
A thought of the bush homestead, and the girl that he left behind.

Then the shearers all sat silent till a man in the corner rose;
Said he, "I've travelled a-plenty but never heard names like those.
Out in the western districts, out in the Castlereagh
Most of the names are easy — short for a man to say.
You've heard of Mungrybambone and the Gundabluey Pine,
Quobbotha, Girilambone, and Terramungamine,
Quambone, Eunonyhareenyha, Wee Waa, and Buntijo—"
But the rest of the shearers stopped him: "For the sake of your jaw, go slow,
If you reckon those names are short ones out where such names prevail,
Just try and remember some long ones before you begin the tale."
And the man from the western district, though never a word he said,
Just winked with his dexter eyelid, and then he retired to bed.

Song of the Future

'Tis strange that in a land so strong,
So strong and bold in mighty youth,
We have no poet's voice of truth
To sing for us a wondrous song.

Our chiefest singer yet has sung
In wild, sweet notes a passing strain,
All carelessly and sadly flung
To that dull world he thought so vain.

"I care for nothing, good nor bad,
My hopes are gone, my pleasures fled,
I am but sifting sand," he said:
What wonder Gordon's songs were sad!

And yet, not always sad and hard;
In cheerful mood and light of heart
He told the tale of Britomarte,
And wrote the Rhyme of Joyous Guard.

And some have said that Nature's face
To us is always sad; but these
Have never felt the smiling grace
Of waving grass and forest trees
On sunlit plains as wide as seas.

"A land where dull Despair is king
O'er scentless flower and songless bird!"
But we have heard the bell-birds ring
Their silver bells at eventide,
Like fairies on the mountain side,
The sweetest note man ever heard.

The wild thrush lifts a note of mirth;
The bronzewing pigeons call and coo
Beside their nests the long day through;
The magpie warbles clear and strong
A joyous, glad, thanksgiving song,
For all God's mercies upon earth.

And many voices such as these
Are joyful sounds for those to tell,
Who know the Bush and love it well,
With all its hidden mysteries.

We cannot love the restless sea,
That rolls and tosses to and fro
Like some fierce creature in its glee;
For human weal or human woe
It has no touch of sympathy.

For us the bush is never sad:
Its myriad voices whisper low,
In tones the bushmen only know,
Its sympathy and welcome glad.

For us the roving breezes bring
From many a blossom-tufted tree —
Where wild bees murmur dreamily —
The honey-laden breath of Spring.

We have no tales of other days,
No bygone history to tell;
Our tales are told where camp-fires blaze
At midnight, when the solemn hush
Of that vast wonderland, the Bush,
Hath laid on every heart its spell.

Although we have no songs of strife,
Of bloodshed reddening the land,

We yet may find achievements grand
Within the bushman's quiet life.

Lift ye your faces to the sky
Ye far blue mountains of the West,
Who lie so peacefully at rest
Enshrouded in a haze of blue;
'Tis hard to feel that years went by
Before the pioneers broke through
Your rocky heights and walls of stone,
And made your secrets all their own.

For years the fertile Western plains
Were hid behind your sullen walls,
Your cliffs and crags and waterfalls
All weatherworn with tropic rains.

Between the mountains and the sea,
Like Israelites with staff in hand,
The people waited restlessly:
They looked towards the mountains old
And saw the sunsets come and go
With gorgeous golden afterglow,
That made the West a fairyland,
And marvelled what that West might be
Of which such wondrous tales were told.

For tales were told of inland seas
Like sullen oceans, salt and dead,
And sandy deserts, white and wan,
Where never trod the foot of man,
Nor bird went winging overhead,
Nor ever stirred a gracious breeze
To wake the silence with its breath —
A land of loneliness and death.

At length the hardy pioneers
By rock and crag found out the way,
And woke with voices of to-day,
A silence kept for years and years.

Upon the Western slope they stood
And saw — a wide expanse of plain
As far as eye could stretch or see
Go rolling westward endlessly.
The native grasses, tall as grain,
Were waved and rippled in the breeze;
From boughs of blossom-laden trees
The parrots answered back again.
They saw the land that it was good,
A land of fatness all untrod,
And gave their silent thanks to God.

The way is won! The way is won!
And straightway from the barren coast
There came a westward-marching host,
That aye and ever onward prest
With eager faces to the West,
Along the pathway of the sun.

The mountains saw them marching by:
They faced the all-consuming drought,
They would not rest in settled land:
But, taking each his life in hand,
Their faces ever westward bent
Beyond the farthest settlement,
Responding to the challenge cry
Of "better country further out."

And lo a miracle! the land
But yesterday was all unknown,
The wild man's boomerang was thrown
Where now great busy cities stand.
It was not much, you say, that these
Should win their way where none withstood;
In sooth there was not much of blood
No war was fought between the seas.

It was not much! but we who know
The strange capricious land they trod —
At times a stricken, parching sod,
At times with raging floods beset —
Through which they found their lonely way,
Are quite content that you should say
It was not much, while we can feel
That nothing in the ages old,
In song or story written yet
On Grecian urn or Roman arch,
Though it should ring with clash of steel,
Could braver histories unfold
Than this bush story, yet untold —
The story of their westward march.

But times are changed, and changes rung
From old to new — the olden days,
The old bush life and all its ways
Are passing from us all unsung.
The freedom, and the hopeful sense
Of toil that brought due recompense,
Of room for all, has passed away,
And lies forgotten with the dead.
Within our streets men cry for bread
In cities built but yesterday.

About us stretches wealth of land,
A boundless wealth of virgin soil
As yet unfruitful and untilled!
Our willing workmen, strong and skilled
Within our cities idle stand,
And cry aloud for leave to toil.

The stunted children come and go
In squalid lanes and alleys black;
We follow but the beaten track
Of other nations, and we grow
In wealth for some — for many, woe.

And it may be that we who live
In this new land apart, beyond
The hard old world grown fierce and fond
And bound by precedent and bond,
May read the riddle right and give
New hope to those who dimly see
That all things may be yet for good,
And teach the world at length to be
One vast united brotherhood.

So may it be, and he who sings
In accents hopeful, clear, and strong,
The glories which that future brings
Shall sing, indeed, a wond'rous song.

The Daylight is Dying

The daylight is dying
    Away in the west,
The wild birds are flying
    In silence to rest;
In leafage and frondage
    Where shadows are deep,
They pass to its bondage —
    The kingdom of sleep.
And watched in their sleeping
    By stars in the height,
They rest in your keeping,
    Oh, wonderful night.

When night doth her glories
    Of starshine unfold,
'Tis then that the stories
    Of bush-land are told.
Unnumbered I hold them
    In memories bright,
But who could unfold them,
    Or read them aright?
Beyond all denials
    The stars in their glories
The breeze in the myalls
    Are part of these stories.
The waving of grasses,
    The song of the river
That sings as it passes
    For ever and ever,
The hobble-chains' rattle,
    The calling of birds,
The lowing of cattle
    Must blend with the words.

Without these, indeed, you
  Would find it ere long,
As though I should read you
  The words of a song
That lamely would linger
  When lacking the rune,
The voice of the singer,
  The lilt of the tune.

But, as one half-hearing
  An old-time refrain,
With memory clearing,
  Recalls it again,
These tales, roughly wrought of
  The bush and its ways,
May call back a thought of
  The wandering days,
And, blending with each
  In the mem'ries that throng,
There haply shall reach
  You some echo of song.

A Ballad of Ducks

The railway rattled and roared and swung
With jolting and bumping trucks.
The sun, like a billiard red ball, hung
In the Western sky: and the tireless tongue
Of the wild-eyed man in the corner told
This terrible tale of the days of old,
And the party that ought to have kept the ducks.
"Well, it ain't all joy bein' on the land
With an overdraft that'd knock you flat;
And the rabbits have pretty well took command;
But the hardest thing for a man to stand
Is the feller who says 'Well I told you so!
You should ha' done this way, don't you know!' —
I could lay a bait for a man like that.

"The grasshoppers struck us in ninety-one
And what they leave — well, it ain't de luxe.
But a growlin' fault-findin' son of a gun
Who'd lent some money to stock our run —
I said they'd eaten what grass we had —
Says he, 'Your management's very bad;
You had a right to have kept some ducks!'

"To have kept some ducks! And the place was white!
Wherever you went you had to tread
On grasshoppers guzzlin' day and night;
And then with a swoosh they rose in flight,
If you didn't look out for yourself they'd fly
Like bullets into your open eye
And knock it out of the back of your head.

"There isn't a turkey or goose or swan,
Or a duck that quacks, or a hen that clucks,
Can make a difference on a run
When a grasshopper plague has once begun;
'If you'd finance us,' I says, 'I'd buy
Ten thousand emus and have a try;
The job,' I says, 'is too big for ducks!

"'You must fetch a duck when you come to stay;
A great big duck — a Muscovy toff —
Ready and fit,' I says, 'for the fray;
And if the grasshoppers come our way
You turn your duck into the lucerne patch,
And I'd be ready to make a match
That the grasshoppers eat his feathers off!"

"He came to visit us by and by,
And it just so happened one day in spring
A kind of cloud came over the sky —
A wall of grasshoppers nine miles high,
And nine miles thick, and nine hundred wide,
Flyin' in regiments, side by side,
And eatin' up every living thing.

"All day long, like a shower of rain,
You'd hear 'em smackin' against the wall,
Tap, tap, tap, on the window pane,
And they'd rise and jump at the house again
Till their crippled carcasses piled outside.
But what did it matter if thousands died —
A million wouldn't be missed at all.

"We were drinkin' grasshoppers — so to speak —
Till we skimmed their carcasses off the spring;
And they fell so thick in the station creek
They choked the waterholes all the week.
There was scarcely room for a trout to rise,
And they'd only take artificial flies —
They got so sick of the real thing.

"An Arctic snowstorm was beat to rags
When the hoppers rose for their morning flight
With the flapping noise like a million flags:
And the kitchen chimney was stuffed with bags
For they'd fall right into the fire, and fry
Till the cook sat down and began to cry —
And never a duck or fowl in sight.

"We strolled across to the railroad track —
Under a cover beneath some trucks,
I sees a feather and hears a quack;
I stoops and I pulls the tarpaulin back —
Every duck in the place was there,
No good to them was the open air.
'Mister,' I says, 'There's your blanky ducks!'"

Ten Little Jackaroos

Ten little Jackaroos at riding wished to shine,
One rode the Corkscrew colt, and then there were nine.

Nine little Jackaroos mending up a gate
One knew how to use the adze — and then there were eight.

Eight little Jackaroos riding home at even
One took a short cut and then there were seven.

Seven little Jackaroos playing up their tricks
One kicked the Boss's dog and then there were six.

Six little Jackaroos learnt to bullock drive
One stroked a bullock's leg and then there were five.

Five little Jackaroos baking in a store
One mistook the arsenic tin and then there were four.

Four little Jackaroos went to fell a tree
One waited till she cracked and then there were three.

Three little Jackaroos feeling rather blue
Started hitting beers to leg, and then there were two.

Two little Jackaroos learnt to fight like fun
One fought the shearer's cook and then there was one.

One little Jackaroo working all alone
He learned some common sense, and then there was none.

The Duties of an Aide-de-Camp

Oh, some folk think vice-royalty is festive and hilarious,
The duties of an A.D.C. are manifold and various,
So listen, whilst I tell in song,
The duties of an *aide-de-cong*.

Whatsoever betide
To the Governor's side
We must stick — or the public would eat him —
For each bounder we see
Says, "Just introduce me
To His Lordship — I'm anxious to meet him."

Then they grab at his paw
And they chatter and jaw
Till they'd talk him to death — if we'd let 'em —
And the folk he has met,
They are all in a fret,
Just for fear he might chance to forget 'em.

When some local King Billy
Is talking him silly,
Or the pound-keeper's wife has waylaid him.
From folks of that stamp
When he has to decamp —
We're his aides to decamp — so we aid him.

Then some feminine beauty
Will come and salute ye,
She may be a Miss or a Madam.
Or a man comes in view
Bails you up, "How de do?"
And you don't know the fellow from Adam.

But you've got to keep sweet
With each man they you meet,
And a trifle like that mustn't bar you,
So you clutch at his fin
And you say with a grin,
"Oh, delighted to see you — how are you?"

Then we do country shows
Where some prize-taker blows
Of his pig — a great, vast forty-stoner —
"See, my Lord! Ain't he fine!
How is that for a swine!"
When it isn't a patch on its owner!

We fix up the dinners
For parsons and sinners
And lawyers and bishops and showmen,
And a judge of the court
We put next to a "sport",
And an Orangeman next to a Roman.

We send invitations
To all celebrations
Some Nobody's presence entreating,
And the old folks of all
We invite to a ball,
And the young — to a grandmothers' meeting.

And when we go dancing,
Like cart-horses prancing,
We plunge where the people are thickenin';
And each gay local swell
Thinks it's "off" to dance well,
So he copies our style — ain't it sickenin'?

Then at banquets we dine
And swig cheap, nasty wine,
But the poor *aide-de-camp* mustn't funk it —
And they call it champagne,
But we're free to maintain
That he feels real pain when he's drunk it.

Then our horses bestriding
We go out a-riding
Lest our health by confinement we'd injure;
You can notice the glare
Of the Governor's hair
When the little boys say, "Go it, Ginger!"

Then some wandering lords —
They so often are frauds —
This out-of-way country invading,
If a man dresses well
And behaves like a swell,
Then he's somebody's cook masquerading.

But an out-and-out ass
With a thirst for a glass
And the symptoms of drink on his "boko",
Who is perpetually
Pursuing the ballet,
He is *always* "the true Orinoko."

We must slave with our quills
Keep the cash — pay the bills —
Keep account of the liquor and victuals —
So I think you'll agree
That the gay A.D.C.
Has a life that's not all beer and skittles.

The Banjo Paterson Trail

BINALONG Binalong, where Paterson went to his first school, is a village of about 250 people, on Burley Griffin Way about 37 kilometres north-west of Yass. It was a major stopping place for Cobb & Co coaches, and Paterson always hoped to witness a 'stick-up'. Not too long before his time, Ben Hall's bushranging gang terrorised the district. The grave of one of his gang, Johnny Gilbert, can be seen on the outskirts of town. Paterson lived with his family at Illalong, on the Yass Road.

BOOKHAM (Bogolong) Bookham is on the Hume Highway about 20 kilometres east of Yass. Originally Bogolong, the village was re-named Bookham by the wife of the Governor of Van Diemens Land, Sir John Franklin. Lady Franklin was travelling overland from Melbourne to Sydney in 1839, and stayed at an inn (now demolished) in the small town. As an adolescent Paterson was taken to a race meeting in Bogolong, which inspired his poem 'Old Pardon the Son of Reprieve'. The site of the Bogolong racetrack is now an open paddock outside the village.

COOMA Originally settled in 1823, Cooma is now the largest town in the Snowy Mountains. It is the town which was the alleged home of the Geebung Polo Club, commemorated by Banjo Paterson in his celebrated poem (see p 146). Known as the gateway to the Snowy Mountains, it is the centre of the Snowy Mountains Hydro-Electric scheme. There is a statue representing the Man from Snowy River, and Paterson, who himself played polo at Cooma, would certainly have known Lambie Street, with its historic buildings. The Mosaic Time Walk in Centennial Park shows life in the Snowy Mountains over the past two hundred years.

CUDAL Rose Barton, 'Banjo' Paterson's mother, was born on her parents' station, Boree Nyrang, about 24 kilometres equidistant from Molong and Orange. Molong first appeared on the maps in 1849 (the name is from the Aboriginal, 'place of many rocks'). It has a beautiful, classified main street and many historical houses. There is a small museum in an early colonial building, once the Golden Fleece hotel, and a stop-over for Cobb & Co coaches before the railway came to the town. There is also a Food, Wine and Cultural centre in what was once Corden's Store, in the main street.

GLADESVILLE The 1830s cottage in which Banjo Paterson lived with his beloved grandmother Emily Barton has been well preserved, with its gardens running down to the Parramatta River, and is now the Banjo Paterson Cottage Restaurant.

ILLALONG Illalong Creek is a locality just off the Burley Griffin Way, about 80 kilometres from Canberra. There appears to be no trace of the Patersons' station, or any indication of its position.

ORANGE 'Banjo' Paterson was born on 17 February 1864 at **Narambla**, on the northern side of Orange, in a house the site of which is marked by an obelisk in Banjo Paterson Park on Ophir Road, 5 kilometres east of Orange. There is also another monument to him in the civic gardens opposite the visitors' centre in Orange itself. Orange officially became a town in 1846, and gold was discovered there in 1851. By the 1870s it was known for its wheat production, but later that century – after the arrival of the railway in 1877 – many orchards were planted (it now produces over half the state's apples). The sixth largest city in New South Wales, it has several fine old houses, and a grand post office and court house, opened in 1880. Cool Park has a delightful little bandstand, set up in 1908, which still has its original gas light fittings.

THE SNOWY MOUNTAINS The Snowy Mountains comprise an area roughly 160 by 80 kilometres, part of the New South Wales section of the Great Dividing Range. Mount Kosciuszko rises to 2228m, the highest point in Australia, and most of the region has been embraced by the Kosciuszko National Park, the largest national park in the state. Despite its name, the Snowy Mountains range is below the snow level, and though during the winter months skiing takes place in many parts of the park, heavy snowfall generally takes place only between June and October. During the summer, bushwalking is popular, as are trout-fishing and mountain-biking. Thredbo, Charlotte Pass, Perisher Valley and Smiggin Holes are extremely popular.

Driving through the Snowy Mountains either from Canberra to the north, from the coast at Bega or from Albury to the west, is an exhilarating experience. Excellent roads connect Bredbo, Cooma, Berridale, Jindabyne, Thredbo, Khancoban, Tumbarumba, Batlow, Tumut and Adaminaby, and from each of these there are byways leading to nearby historic settlements. Admirers of the film of The Man from Snowy River will have no difficulty in recognising some of the places where it was made.

SYDNEY The buildings in which Paterson practised law have all been demolished. Returning from the Boer War, he gave a series of lectures in **Centennial** Hall, which had only then been open for eleven years, and was at the time the largest hall of its kind in the British Empire. Its massive ceiling is of moulded zinc, its stained glass windows show Australian flora, and its floor is made of Tasmanian blackwood and tallowwood. It also has of course an enormous organ.

WEE JASPER Wee Jasper, just across the Goodradigbee River from Paterson's property, Coodra Vale, is still a small village - near the Burrinjuck Dam and about an hour's motoring from Yass. The Wee Jasper reserves embrace both the Goodradigbee River and Micalong Creek.

WINTON Originally known as Pelican Waterhole, Winton was re-named in 1879 by the local postmaster who, it is said, got tired of writing the longer name. He happened to come from an English Winton, a suburb of Bournemouth. It now advertises itself as 'the town where "Waltzing Matilda" was written'. Not entirely true (see p.3 and 37) – the ruins of the station at Dagworth, where the song was born, are about 100 kilometres north-west of the town. They can be visited with permission from the Australian Pastoral Company (web address **www.napco.com.au**).

The Combo Waterhole, events at which are said to have sparked off the verses, is on Belfast Station, 145 kilometres north-west of Winton. Combo is just south of Kynuna and 132kilometres north-west of Winton. Turn south off the Landsborough Highway 13 kilometres south of Kynuna. A four-wheel-drive is recommended, but in any event vehicles are not allowed beyond the car park. The 2.6 kilometres walk to the Waterhole is not arduous. The track begins at the car park and crosses the Diamantina River's braided channels. The track should not be crossed if flooded.

In Winton itself is the Waltzing Matilda Centre, with life-size models of swagmen and troopers under a coolabah tree. There is a 'Home of the Legend' room and a light and sound show as well as the Quantilda Museum which highlights the life of the pioneers. There is also a Visitors' Centre – see **www.matildacentre.com.au**.

YASS Yass, near which Banjo Paterson lived as a child, is mainly celebrated as the home of the explorer Hamilton Hume, whose home is preserved. It is a handsome town with some fine classical buildings along the main street, once on the main road from Sydney to Melbourne. The courthouse and CBC bank, with its hitching posts, are especially notable, as is the station with the shortest platform in Australia.

Sources

For Paterson's own work the primary source must be the two volumes edited by his granddaughters, Rosamund Campbell and Philippa Harvie, and published by the Lansdowne Press in Sydney in 1983. I have attempted to contact the editors, but without success; they have been made aware however of the preparation of this book, and I am happy to acknowledge here the invaluable nature of the tremendous and painstaking work they did in collecting together all that is known of A. B. Paterson's journalism, fiction and verse.

There have been two previous biographies – Clement Semmler's *The Banjo of the Bush* (University of Queensland Press, Queensland, 1966) and Colin Roderick's *Banjo Paterson: poet by accident* (Allen & Unwin, St Leonards, 1993). The latter, in particular, is extremely comprehensive, and it is difficult to suppose that the author failed to record any significant details of Paterson's life. I am extremely indebted to both these publications.

In addition I must record my thanks to the Mitchell Library (in particular to Ms Maria Wiemers) and the Mosman Library. Mr Roger Clarke maintains an excellent 'Banjo Paterson' page on the Net at **www.anu.edu.au/people/Roger.Clark**. Another useful web site is **www.nla.gov.au/epubs/waltzingmatilda/1-Orig-FirstManuscript**.

Notes

Chapter One

1. *Sydney Morning Herald*, 4 February-4 March 1939
2. *On Kiley's Run*, stanza 8
3. *The Animals Noah Forgot*, Prologue: *The Plains*
4. *Sydney Morning Herald*, Ibid.
5. *Ibid*
6. *Ibid* and see p.130
7. 'My various schools' in *The Sydneian* magazine, May 1890.
8. *Sydney Morning Herald*, Ibid.
9. *The Bulletin*, 18 May 1895

Chapter Two

10. *Sydney Morning Herald*, February 4, 1939
11. *Australia for the Australians – a political pamphlet showing the necessity for Land Reform combined with Protection* (Gordon & Gotch, Sydney, 1889)
12. '*The Hyponotist*', *The Bulletin*, 19 July 1890.
13. *The Bulletin*, February 1885.
14. *The Bulletin*, 30 October 1886
15. *The Bulletin*, 25 December 1886
16. *The Bulletin*, 24 December 1892
17. He was hardly ever referred to in print as simply 'Banjo', but always 'The Banjo', and I have maintained that usage.
18. See p.144
19. See p.128
20. See p.128
21. *The Sydney Mail, December 1938*
22. Allen & Unwin, 1993
23. *Sydney Morning Herald*, 11 February 1939
24. 'In Defence of the Bush', *The Bulletin*, 23 July 1892

25. Quoted Semmler, C., *The Banjo of the Bush* (University of Queensland Press, 1966) at p.126. *brumbies*: free-roaming, feral horses. *Mulga* – shrubland. *brigalow* – wattle.
26. Published in 'The Man from Snowy River', 20 October 1895
27. *The Bulletin*, 20 October 1895
28. *Sunday Morning Herald*, 11 February 1939
29. See p.146

Chapter Three

30. See p.3
31. See p.174
32. *The Bulletin*, 31 December 1898

Chapter Four

33. *The Bulletin*, 19 May 1900. The Editor substituted 'blessed' for 'bloody'.
34. Paterson, A. B., Happy Dispatches (Lansdowne Press, Sydney, 1980) at p.37
35. *Sydney Morning Herald*, 18 November 1899
36. *Sydney Morning Herald*, 6 December 1899. Milner was spoken of as a possible future Governor-General of Australia; but that was a 'big job' he did not get.
37. *Ibid*.
38. *Happy Dispatches*, Op. cit., pp.40-43
39. *The Bulletin*, 4 November 1899
40. Paterson, A. B., *Singer of the Bush* (ed. Campbell, R. and Harvie, P., Lansdowne Press, Sydney, 1983) p.471
41. *Sydney Morning Herald*, 17 February, 1900
42. *Ibid*
43. *Happy Dispatches*, op. cit., p.72
44. 'Horses in Warfare', The Story of South Africa, 1899. Paterson, A. B., Song of the Pen (ed. Campbell, R. and Harvie, P., Lansdowne Press, Sydney, 1983) pp.69-70
45. *Sydney Morning Herald*, 11 August 1900
46. *Sydney Bulletin*, 14 February 1941

47. Laager – a defensive encampment
48. *Sydney Morning Herald*, 2 April 1900
49. *Singer of the Bush*, p.542
50. *Sydney Morning Herald*, 2 April 1900
51. *Singer of the Bush*, op. cit., p.535
52. *Happy Dispatches*, op. cit., pp.47-8
53. *Ibid.*
54. *Sydney Morning Herald*, 16 March 1900
55. *Singer of the Bush*, op. cit., p.582
56. *Song of the Pen*, op. cit., pp.598-601
57. *Happy Dispatches* in Song of the Pen, p.593
58. *Sydney Morning Herald*, 29 September 1900
59. *Rio Grande's Last Race and Other Verses*, 1902
60. *Sydney Morning Herald*, 21 July 1900
61. Exeter Hall - a building in London at which meetings of the anti-slavery league were regularly held; 'Exeter Hall' became a synonym for the Anti-Slavery lobby.

Chapter Five

62. *Singer of the Bush*, p.xiv
63. *Song of the Pen*, op. cit., p.14
64. *Song of the Pen*, p.37
65. See p.165
66. *Song of the Pen*, p.37
67. *Song of the Pen*, pp.630-34
68. *Song of the Pen*, p.54
69. 'Lay of the Motor Car', *Song of the Pen*, p.53
70. *Song of the Pen*, p.142
71. *Song of the Pen*, p.476

Chapter Six

72. Roderick, Colin, *Banjo* Allen & Unwin 1992 p.182
73. *Sydney Evening News*, February 1905
74. *Song of the Pen*, op. cit. p.252
75. *Evening News*, December 1913
76. *Ibid*

77. *Saltbush Bill, J.P., and other verses*, 1917

Chapter Seven

78. *Song of the Pen*, op. cit., p. 364
79. *Happy Dispatches*, op. cit., p.93
80. Lyddite was a form of high explosive composed of molten and cast picric acid, widely used during both the Boer War and First World War.
81. *Sydney Morning Herald*, 15 September 1914
82. *Happy Dispatches*, op. cit., p.108-9
83. *Ibid.*, pp.58-9
84. I*bid.*, pp.121-2
85. 'The Army Mules' - *The Kia-Ora Cooee*, March 1918
86. *Happy Dispatches*, op.cit., p.131
87. *War in the Garden of Eden*, New York, 1919, Chapter VIII

Chapter Eight

88. *Song of the Pen*, op. cit., p.743
89. *Sydney Mail*, 7 January 1899
90. *The Sydney Sportsman*, 31 July 1923
91. *The Sydney Sportsman*, 24 April 1923
92. *Song of the Pen*, op. cit, p.685
93. 'The Road to Old Man's Town', *Rio Grande's Last Race* (1920)

Chapter Nine

94. A Nervous Governor-General, *The Evening News*, January 1904
95. *The Bulletin*, August 1892
96. *The Bulletin*, August 1892
97. *The Sydney Sportsman*, July 1923
98. Producing an Australian Popular Music (*Journal of Australian Studies*, January 2007)

INDEX

'Geebung Polo Club', 34; 'Hypnotist, the', 24; 'Job for McGuinness, A, 129-30; 'Last Parade', 66-7; 'Lay of the Motor Car', 82; 'Man from Snowy River', 28; 'Mountain Squatter', 107-8; 'Mylora Elopement', 25-6; 'Old Australian Ways', 83-4'On Riley's Run', 7; 'Pardon, the son of Reprieve', 12; 'Road to Old Man's Town', 136-7; 'Song of the Wheat', 110; 'Under the Shadow of Kiley's Hill', 30-1; 'We're All Australians Now', 118; 'With French to Kimberley', 64-5; Books: Australia for the Australians, 20ff.; The Man from Snowy River, 38ff, 89, 131; In No Man's Land, 73; Rio Grande's Last Race, 89; An Outback Marriage, 98; Old Bush Songs (editor), 99-100; Saltbush Bill, J.P., 125; Three Elephant Power, 125; The Cook's Dog, 125; Collected Verse, 125, 130; The Shearer's Colt, 126-7, 135; Racehorses and Racing, 127; Animals Noah Forgot, 132-4; Happy Dispatches, 134
Paterson, Hugh Barton (son), 95
Paterson, Grace (daughter), 95
Paterson, John (brother), 5
Paterson, Rose (mother), 5, 17
Pink Un, The, 82
Popler Grove, 60
Port Elizabeth, 43
Queensland, 75

R-S-T
radio, 131-1
Randam, 48
Randwick, 126
Remount Service, 117ff
Rensburg, 48
Reynold's Weekly, 71
Rhodes, Cecil, 57
Riley, Frederick Whistler, 2, 35
Riley, Sarah Ann, 2, 28, 35-37
Roberts, Frederick Sleigh, Earl, 48-9, 57-89, 60, 72
Robertson, George, 35, 38, 73, 81, 103, 109, 125, 130
Rockend Stone Cottage, see Gladesville
Rockhampton, 75
Roderick, Colin, 28
Roosevelt, Kermit, 122-3
Rottingdean, 82
'Rule 303', 92
Russell, William, 1
Schreiner, Olive, 49
Searle, Harry, 14
Shanghai, 76

Skinner, Harrie, 97
Slingersfortein, 48
Smith's Weekly, 125
Smith, Sir Joynton, 125
Spain and Salway, 17, 19
Spectator, The, 38-9
Sportsman, The, 126
Stainburn Downs, 6-7
Steel, H. Peden, 35
Street, John William, 23, 28
Swinburne, A. C., 17, 140-2
Sydney Grammar School, 12-13
Sydney Evening News, 93ff
Sydney Mail, The, 27, 28, 73, 137
Sydney Morning Herald, The, 5, 40, 73, 84, 87, 111, 137
Tennyson, Alfred Lord, 141, 144
Tenterfield, 94
The Times, 38
Tianjin, 74
Tompson, Charles, 138
Town and Country Journal, The, 103
Trickett, Ned, 14
trout fishing, 105

V-W-Y
Van Beuren, Trooper, 92
Vila, 85
Walker, Alice Emily, see Paterson, Alice
Warrnambool, 2, 35-6
Wee Jasper, 103
Westminster, Duchess of, 45-6
Williams, Col. W. D. C., 43
Wimereux, 115
Winton, 2, 35
Witton, George, 91
Wood, Harry, 2
Woollahra, 125
Yangtze, the, 76
Yantai, see Cheefoo
Yass, 7, 104, 188
Yellow Peril, 74
Yeoval, 5
York, H.R.H. Duke of, 81

ALSO BY DEREK PARKER

and available from Woodslane Press

OUTBACK
The Discovery of Australia's Interior

In 1800, while the coast of Australia had finally been charted, the vast interior of the continent, and routes across its deserts and mountains from north to south and east to west lay all undiscovered. By 1874, its lands had been all but won. Derek Parker's exciting book gathers together the stories of those intrepid explorers who, often against great odds, on journeys of months or even years, beat starvation, inadequate information and mapping, disease and loss, to forge a routes which would enable the country's development. From early explorers, who were generally escaped convicts, to the son of a Lincolnshire surgeon who coined the name 'Australia'; from explorers Major Mitchell, who slaughtered aborigines, to Sir George Grey, who learnt their language, recorded their culture and came to love and understand them; and from the greatest overland expedition in Australian history in 1844 to continued failed attempts to find a mythical 'inland sea', this is a fascinating read.

Paperback $24.95 ISBN: 9781921203923
Available September 2009

ALSO BY DEREK PARKER

and available from Woodslane Press

ARTHUR PHILLIP
Australia's First Governor

Over the two centuries since his appointment, commentators have been as surprised at the choice of Arthur Phillip as Governor of the new penal colony at New South Wales as some were at the time (the First Lord of the Admiralty, to mention only the most distinguished critic). But was it really so surprising? What did the Home Office and the Admiralty expect of a man who was to navigate a fleet to the antipodes, and when he got it there unload its cargo of unregenerate criminals and forge them into some sort of a working colony? Apart from the necessary seamanship, they needed a man with a cool head who understood men and how to control them, a man capable of governing himself, possessed of calm and understanding and a thorough grasp of reality, with complete loyalty to the Crown and Government and a determination to plan and carry through an enterprise unlike any other within living memory. Fortunately, there were one or two men at the Admiralty who understood that Arthur Phillip possessed all these credentials. This new biography covers Phillip's whole life, but has a particular focus on his selection for the role of Governor, the preparation of the first fleet, the journey from England, the establishment of the colony and Phillip's governorship.

Hardback $44.95 ISBN: 9781921203992
Paperback $24.95 ISBN: 9781921683480

ALSO BY DEREK PARKER

and available from Woodslane Press

GOVERNOR MACQUARIE
His life, times and revolutionary vision for Australia

The first new biography of Lachlan Macquarie in decades, this book draws on a wealth of sources, both in Australia and overseas, to paint a picture of the man and his times. It must be seen as one of the great ironies of Australian history that, as far as the British Government was concerned, he failed in his duty as Governor of New South Wales - as was clearly documented to official minds in the official report compiled by Commissioner John Bigge. This report concluded that while Governor Macquarie had certainly supervised the building in New South Wales of some good roads and some handsome buildings (if at far too high a cost to the British taxpayers), under his government the colony had ceased to be what it was required to be: a place with a reputation for cruelty and hopelessness so terrifying that the very threat of being banished there would strike terror into the heart of any prospective malefactor. Macquarie had in fact a vision shared by few others that New South Wales – indeed the whole of New Holland - had the potential to become 'one of the greatest and most flourishing colonies belonging to the British Empire', and became determined to do his part in steering the fledgling community in that direction.

Paperback $24.95 ISBN: 9781921606915

ALSO AVAILABLE FROM WOODSLANE PRESS

BLIGH IN AUSTRALIA
A new appraisal of William Bligh and the Rum Rebellion

By Russell Earls Davies

The Rum Rebellion has, for generations, been told to school children as one of the better stories of Australian History - how Bligh, the villain of Hollywood's version of the Bounty mutiny story, was a tyrant deposed by the New South Wales Corps and dragged out from his hiding place under a bed. It has even been said – and this is just as far from the truth - that the overthrowing of Governor Bligh was a victory for democracy and colonial self-government. Although there have been two excellent, scholarly works that have told the truth about the Rum Rebellion, one focuses very much on the overall story of the time, while the other focuses on the legal situation prevailing. Neither combines the historical with the legal situation and presents a good story in which a number of interesting characters played a significant role. Considering that some historians have failed to understand the legal aspects of the events that led up to the Rum Rebellion and have been unfairly prejudiced against Bligh and in favour of John Macarthur, Russell Earl Davies has endeavoured to present an account of Bligh's time in Australia that, as far as possible from the available evidence, tells what actually did happen. Bligh in Australia lends impetus to the growing recent trend to recognise that William Bligh was no tyrant or coward, as his mutinous enemies alleged, but an incredibly strong-willed servant of the British Government who did exactly as he had been ordered. On the Bounty and in New South Wales he faced situations where the forces against him would have utterly defeated a lesser man, yet in the end he prevailed.

Paperback $24.95 ISBN: 9781921683503

ALSO AVAILABLE FROM WOODSLANE PRESS

THIS ACCURSED LAND
Douglas Mawson's incredible Antarctic journey

By Lennard Bickel

Antarctica is not generally friendly to life, and is aggressively hostile to human life, and yet for the last 150 years explorers have pitted themselves against it time and again. Frequently, and particularly during the 'heroic' age of the first couple of decades of the twentieth century, their efforts were met with extreme danger and even death. The names Scott, Shackleton and Amundsen are writ especially large in our cultural history because of their harrowing journeys to the ice continent. Douglas Mawson's name does not shine quite as brightly, which ironically gives him much credit: he was not so much a 'pole-chaser' as a committed scientist, and won more secrets from Antarctica than his more famous contemporaries put together; and careful planning meant that he usually suffered less from the mishaps that plagued others. And yet, just once, catastrophe did strike. Three hundred miles from base-camp - three hundred miles of the coldest, most lethal territory on earth - Mawson lost one of his two companions and most of his supplies down a crevasse. Soon after the survivors' attempt to claw back to base began, his other companion died of the horrendous conditions they had to bear. This disaster, and Mawon's incredible 6-week solo journey back to base - described by Sir Edmund Hilary as the greatest story of lone survival in polar exploration - make up the thrilling narrative of Lennard Bickel's classic book.

Paperback $29.95 ISBN: 9781921683046